In the Loop: Radical Potholder Patterns & Techniques

In the Loop: Radical Potholder Patterns & Techniques

by
Deborah Jean Cohen

and
Mary Clarke
Yavia Mirez
Christine Olsen Reis
Bill West
Angela West

Copyright © 2021 Deborah Jean Cohen

Apollo's Lyre, Box Chains, Boxed Angles, Circuitboard, Diamonds Are Forever, Exposed Filmstrips, Garden Path, Greek Half Key, Little Squares/Thor's Hammer, Looking Through Barred Windows, Maze in a Diamond, Maze of Enigma, Multicursal Maze, Shadow Baseball Diamond, Shadow Zigzag, Shine Bright Like a Diamond, Square Maze, Up the Down Staircase, Vessel III, Wavy Zigzag, and Wiggle Worms charts used by permission of William West.

Christine's Garden Sampler, Diamond Mix, Diamond Rose, Escape, Infinite, Loop de Loop, Opening, and Shadow Cross charts used by permission of Christine Olsen Reis.

Facets, Fillet, Ramble, Right Angles, Right-angle Hitch, and Straight-edged Spiral charts used by permission of Mary Clarke.

Bernie's Mitts chart used by permission of Yavia Mirez.

Birds Flying High chart used by permission of Angela West.

All rights reserved. No part of this book may be transmitted or reproduced in any form or by any means without the prior written permission of the copyright holder.

Third Edition

ISBN 978-1-7368576-0-1 (coil bound)
ISBN 978-1-7368576-2-5 (trade paperback)
Library of Congress Control Number: 2021911863

Printed in the United States of America
Bàghban House Fort Smith 2021
baghbanhouse@gmail.com

Cover design: Evelyn Nelson
Cover photographs: Jack Kulawik
Front cover: "Foghorn" woven by Christine Olsen Reis
Back cover: "Lockdown Lines" woven by Christine Olsen Reis

Special thanks to Evelyn Nelson for invaluable technical assistance.

to
all potholder weavers,
all weavers everywhere,
and to
Martin

TABLE OF CONTENTS

INTRODUCTION		p. 1
CHAPTER 1	how to use this book; tips; tools; sources	p. 2
CHAPTER 2	how to chart a potholder from scratch	p. 14
CHAPTER 3	potholder patterns: plain weave	p. 26
CHAPTER 4	potholder patterns: shadow weave	p. 59
CHAPTER 5	potholder patterns: twill	p. 123
CHAPTER 6	a somewhat nerdy log cabin study	p. 160
CHAPTER 7	potholder weavers	p. 169
GLOSSARY		p. 184
INDEX	pattern list in alphabetical order	p. 186

Introduction

This book was born from the dearth of available potholder patterns, the lockdown of 2020, and Noreen Crone-Findlay's original potholder pattern 'Stepping Stones'. I admired Stepping Stones, and the proverbial lightbulb went off when I found a 4-harness weaving draft online. (That draft became Spiral Maze.) I charted it for the potholder loom: it took a long time to chart, so I analyzed what was happening and developed a method to chart any draft. Suddenly there were unlimited possible potholder patterns. I wanted to make a book. Kate Kilmurray invited me to present the charting method at a meeting of her Weaving Way Community, and there I asked for help: I needed test weavers. I got more than test weavers: I got a group of artists and designers who became the co-authors of this book, and expanded my nebulous idea in a way I could not have imagined. I'd met Bill West even before the meeting. He had been charting from weaving drafts months before I began; his converted charts and original designs are a staple of this book. Angela, his sister, came along with Bill as a test weaver and discoverer of Birds Flying High. Mary Clarke had been designing for years: here you will find her iconic patterns and distinctive style. Christine Olsen Reis, who had been weaving potholders into art throughout the lockdown, test wove, then became a strong designer. Yavia Mirez (Bernie's Mitts) emanated support, and tirelessly wove. Each person seemed to catalyze the other: it is a dynamic group.

My picture.

Here you will find the results of that group, the Potholder Weavers. Converted charts, original designs, and a collection of strong classic potholder patterns are collected together for your weaving library, and for your creative energy.

Tertön Lama Hyolmo asked me to fundraise for a monastery being built in a remote area of Nepal: Illam. The monastery, Thegtse Sangyé Chöling, will be the source of education, community support, and senior care for the area. All proceeds of this book's sale are donated to its construction. Please search for Facebook username @ThegtseSangyeCholing, scroll to the bottom of the posts, and you can follow progress from the beginning.

— Deborah Jean Cohen **Instagram: @deborahjeancohen @radicalpotholderweavers**

CHAPTER 1

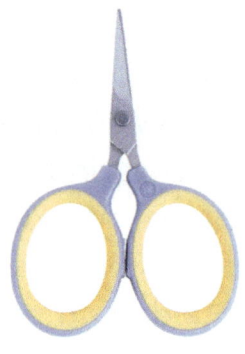

reading patterns; tips; techniques; sources

Welcome to potholder weaving! In this chapter you will find useful weaving tips, tricks, tools, sources, and some oddball techniques.

HOW TO READ THE PATTERNS Pattern notation in this book follows this rule: '—' means weave your weft loop **over** the warp loop, and '|' means weave the weft loop **under** the warp loop. Warp column numbers are marked at the bottom of the chart, and weft rows at the right side. Warp colors are at the top, and weft on the left side. The generic placeholders A and B are used for the colors. <u>A is always gray, and B is always white in all of the charts.</u>

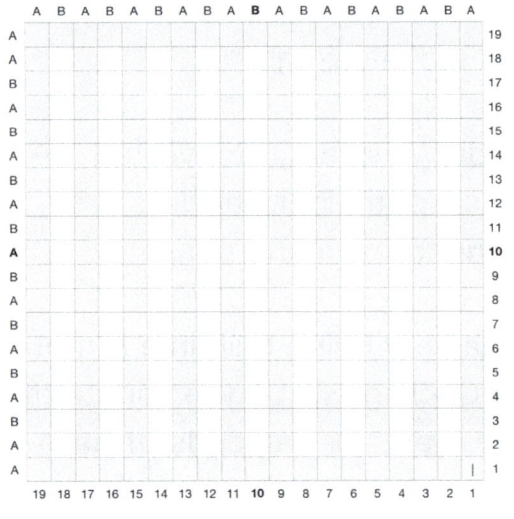

Weave II

For plain weave charts, the Harrisville Designs Potholder Wizard convention is followed, except that here the lower right-hand square is marked with the beginning pick direction. In the example to the left, the first pick is under, so you would weave under/over until the row's end, then over/under for the next row, and so on.

> Please note that patterns which are symmetrical around a column are charted for the 19 and 27 peg looms; those symmetrical around a line are charted for the 18 and 28 peg looms. If you have only the traditional 18 and 27 peg looms, drop a column and a row for those patterns that are charted for the 19 and 28 peg looms. Non-symmetrical patterns are charted for the traditional loom sizes.

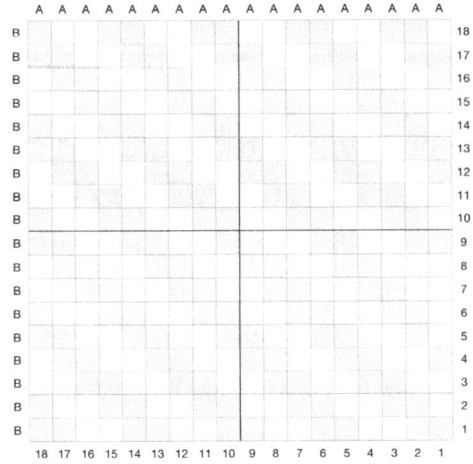

Basic twill.

Basic twill always has the warp all one color, and the weft all another. So, when the weft loop is woven under the warp loop, the warp color shows; and when the weft loop is woven over the warp loop, the weft color shows. In all the basic twill charts here, gray is under and white is over. In the chart to the left, you see that the first row is woven under/under, over/over and so on until the end of the row. The next row reads first over, then under/under, over/over until the last square, which is an under. This tends to weave up very quickly, because your eye immediately translates the weaving direction into motion.

The other pattern types in this book, shadow weave and predominantly twill structures (which I've placed in the twill chapter), are straightforward. Each square will contain the weaving direction, under (|) or over (—). 2- and 3-floats are bolded red, to make them easier to pick out; if they predominate, then single picks are bolded.

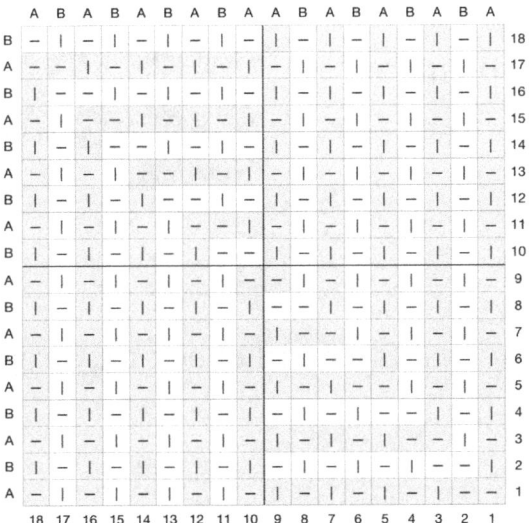

Shadow weave.

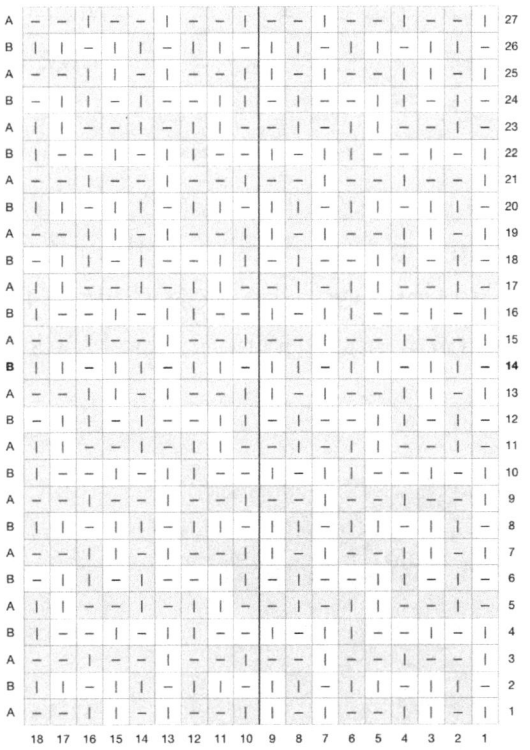

Predominately twill.

3

TIPS

symmetry around a column on an 18 peg loom

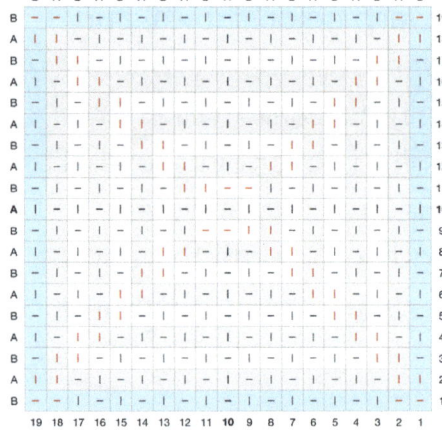

Many designs in this book are symmetrical around a column: these are charted for the 19 or 27 peg loom. Dropping a column and a row will fit a 19-peg design on an 18 peg loom, but symmetry is lost. For those of you who might be unhappy with that situation, drop the first and last rows and the first and last columns of the chart, and weave on 17 pegs of your 18 peg loom.

weaving — making a shed, evening out take-up, and straight rows

If you weave first with a knitting needle, it's easy to slide your hook through the shed made by the needle. It's faster to weave that way, and if you happen to put the wrong color loop in, or change your mind, you don't have to reweave.

Laying your loop in an arch within the shed evens out the take-up that occurs in the interlacing of warp and weft as you beat the weft down. The weave will be more consistent, and the need for blocking reduced.

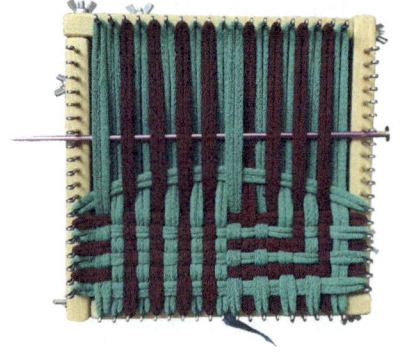

The knitting needle is also a good check for straight rows!

And a knitting needle or chopstick across the bottom provides a strong base to keep rows straight as you beat them down. This tip is from Christine, and I use it regularly. I sometimes add a gum band (rubber band to you who are not from Western Pennsylvania), which holds the knitting needle firmly against the pegs.

maintaining tension when crocheting off

It's far easier to crochet the potholder off the loom if the loops are tensioned. Use bullnose clips as you go along: loops won't pop off.
(Note the yarn tied around the loom at the bottom — I mark the middle of mine, on the bottom and usually the right side. Others mark every so many pegs. This makes it easier to track row and column count.

blocking

Potholders straight off the loom aren't square. Several things can cause that: uneven weaving; loops that are of different lengths, thickness, material or springiness; the potholder pattern itself. You can mitigate that by careful weaving, matching the loops as best you can, and by stretching each loop well before placing on the warp pegs or weaving in the weft loop. I tug each Harrisville Designs loop just until I hear the fabric crack (though not all of them will crack), and stretch each Wool Novelty Company loop until they are barely tensioned over the loom. I do the best I can with Pepperell — some stretch and some do not. Stretching allows the warp and weft room to interlace nicely, reducing take-up, and allowing your fabric to lay flat. Still, even with nicely stretched and matched loops, and careful weaving, potholders seldom come off the loom perfectly square. To me, this is just one of their endearing qualities, and I'm happy giving them a few tugs and calling it a day. But if you want to give them as a gift, or you just have to have them as square as possible, you can block them.

Blocking is a method to adjust the shape of the finished piece, setting the final dimensions of the woven fabric. If you're a knitter, you'll be familiar with the idea; blocking potholders is very similar. There are many different ways to block.

Figure 1

* Press with a steam iron.
* Spray with water, and pin to a grid (Figure 1) until dry. Leave the potholder on the loom overnight.

There are some variations to the 'leave it on the loom' method: I soak my 27 and 28 peg potholders with very hot water while still on the loom, blot them, carefully dry the loom, and dry in front of a fan, generally overnight.

Bill places small bullnose clips (Figure 2) on his potholders after crocheting off each side, then leaves it on the loom overnight. This method puts very precise corners on the potholder.

Figure 2

SOURCES
loops

Potholders made with loops owe their existence to the hosiery industry: sock mills produce huge amounts of "cut off strips", made as the sock tubing is cut. In the depression era 1930's, as a way to use this waste, mills would package these "loopers" with a loom and sell them to housewives. Today loops still come from sock mills.

There are many resellers of loops, but listed here are the sources:

Harrisville Designs, Harrisville, NH

Harrisville Designs custom makes and dyes their loops from recycled yarn — they aren't sock mill waste. These are the most consistent loops on the market today, though variation still occurs: like yarn, color will not be exact from dye lot to dye lot, and loop stretchiness can also vary. Harrisville Designs carries traditional loops and the larger PRO size, meant for a 10" loom. There's a wide selection of colors — 32 plus black and white — in their Brights, Pastels, and Contemporary lines. Excellent customer service. Harrisville Designs loops are the basic tools in our loop toolkit: with their wonderful color palette and consistency, they're the go-to loop.

Wool Novelty Company, Levittown, NY

Wool Novelty Company dyes and packages cotton loops from sock mills. These are sturdy loops, vary in size and color within each dye lot, and come in 10 colors plus black and natural. Most will fit the traditional 7" loom, and save the others for your 13- or 14-peg loom. Extraordinary customer service. We love these loops for their variation and wonderful saturated colors: their light greens are an incredible acid color; the darker blues wonderful shades of denim; their black amazing (try a black-on-black pattern using both Harrisville Designs and WNC blacks); their browns and natural often shot through with black or light lycra. Use WNC with other brands' loops: adding a sturdier loop to your mix will stabilize the more complex patterns, often making the blocking step unnecessary. And mixing WNC with Pepperell or Hillcreek Fiber Studio's wool loops does much to cure take-up. Above right: Mary Clarke's Fillet pattern, woven by her, in WNC brown, blue, and natural.

Pepperell Braiding Company, Pepperell, MA

Pepperell has 3 factories: in Pepperell, MA, Bradford, PA, and Ningbo, China. They sell a 1# bag of "mixed artificial fibers" but the loops have a distinctly natural feel. I'm wondering if some of them contain modal. The loops are all over the map — most fit the 7" traditional loom, others the 13- and 14-peg loom, and a very few are so tiny I'm saving them for my 9-peg pin loom. The colors are random. You never know what you'll get — all variegated, some with shiny metallic threads mixed in. I absolutely love some of their shades, and absolutely hate others. (I overdye those.) But many of my most favorite potholders are made with Pepperell loops: they're one of a kind. Above left: the Broken Comb pattern, woven in Harrisville Designs Carnation and Pepperell shades of brown and orange.

> Note: We don't recommend using polyester or nylon loops for potholders that will be used in the kitchen. These fibers melt when exposed to heat. They can, though, be safely used for potholder trivets, rugs, boxes, or purses. However, I use my potholders made with mixed Pepperell and Harrisville Designs or WNC loops in the kitchen, though I don't hold them over an open flame. Be cautious.

Solmate Socks, Hickory, NC

An obvious way to get your loops is from a sock mill. Solmate is a sock mill, and as part of their sustainable production ethic, packs the cotton loopers raw right off the factory floor, masses of extraneous threads and all, into a carton, and will give it to you if you pay postage. The carton weighs 60#. Colors are random: the waste from whatever sock run is happening. So I estimate that about 1/3 of my box contains white loops shot through with black lycra, a good deal of the rest dark loops (lots of charcoal gray), and the remainder various colors. Yavia's box was a majority red and blue. The loops are raggedy and rather thick, have lots of threads, and are a bit harder to weave with. They're worth the effort: they add texture, structure and a different color palette to your work. Solmate has extraordinary customer service!

 This is Open Cross, which is simply the reverse side of Square-in-a-Square. It's woven in Harrisville Designs Black and Solmate colors on a 19-peg loom.

Now, if you for some strange reason don't want 60# of loopers, you can get Solmate loops from:

Homestead Weaving Studio LLC, Columbus, IN

Homestead Weaving does the sorting and cleanup for you, and packages traditional, jumbo and baby Solmate loops in half-pound to 3# bags. Baby loops are available packed in a kit with a very well made loom (12 pegs), custom built to accommodate Solmate's thicker width. They also sell kits with loops and looms in traditional (16 peg), jumbo (20 peg), and hybrid (16x20 peg) sizes, and have added even more loom sizes. Plus, you can choose the colors you want: by individual color or their own selected custom blends. I have 3 of their kits, and am happy with them. The pegs are cotter pins. (More on cotter pins later.) NOTE: you can weave Solmate loops on the more common 18- and 27-peg looms, so feel free to experiment.

As far as I know, these are the root sources of every cotton or mixed fiber loop in the United States. There's one source for wool loops:

Carol Leigh's Hillcreek Fiber Studio, Columbia, MO

In earlier literature which came along with your Hillcreek order, Harrisville Designs is listed as the source of undyed wool loops, both traditional and PRO sized. My latest order didn't include that information, and Harrisville Designs does not offer wool loops to the general public. Carol Leigh is famous for her colorfast pokeberry dye recipe: colorfast it is; the wool I dyed using it is bright after 6 years. Carol dyes wool loops with poke, and other natural dyestuff, and provides undyed loops as well. They are expensive, but the price, considering the labor that goes along with dyeing naturally, is very fair. You can choose among 24 truly luscious shades, or Carol's custom collections. Frankly I love wool potholders. They weave up beautifully, and have a wonderful hand. Wool, unlike cotton, has a memory: so take-up, or draw-in, is more pronounced and your potholder will be distinctly smaller. Below is a size comparison — cotton vs mostly wool. You can see the difference!

**Left: Harrisville Designs Red and White
Right: WNC red and Hillcreek denim.
Woven by Mary Clarke on an 18 peg loom.**

looms

All the loop sources listed above carry looms. There are so many loom makers, and resellers of metal looms, that I can't list them all. I use and recommend Cottage Looms Designs on Etsy. Rebecca and her husband Rick make sturdy wooden looms with cotter pin pegs. Unlike metal looms, wood looms stand up well to the tension of loops strung across them, and don't warp. The cotter pin pegs are long, so that your loops don't randomly pop off; they're rounded, so don't stab your wrists; and they're very sturdy and won't break like wood pegs or bend like nails. The infamous Last Row is much easier to weave: just slide the loops up the pegs — your hook will slide right through. They carry 18- and 19-peg and 27- and 28-peg looms, plus an 18x27 peg oblong loom. Rebecca and Rick will make custom looms, and are the source of my 13- and 14-peg coaster looms. Cottage Looms Designs' prices are very fair, and they're extremely nice people — extraordinary customer service.

HOW TO MAKE YOUR OWN LOOPS FROM SOCKS

Cut the socks at the red lines.

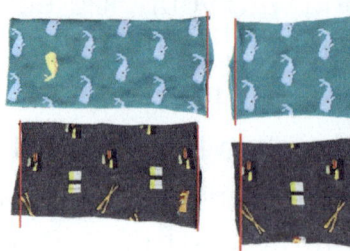

Trim them up so the tubes have straight ends.

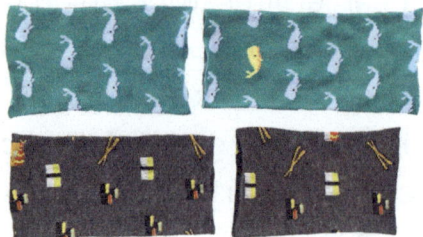

Then, cut each tube into 3/8" strips.

They'll look like this when cut.

After cutting, the loops naturally curl up, with the inside of the sock showing.

Right Angles woven with Harrisville Turquoise and sock loops.

AN EXAMPLE OF TAKE-UP, aka DRAW-IN

Each potholder above is woven with Harrisville loops on an 18-peg loom.
Left: plain weave   Center: twill (2-floats)   Right: a 3-float basket weave
You can see how weaving over/under 2 and 3 warp loops results in progressively smaller potholders. These patterns are balanced: the floats occur evenly across the loom. When a pattern has 3-floats in only a few areas, draw-in can occur unevenly, and may require blocking.

SPLIT-LOOP TECHNIQUE

Normal potholder weaving views the warp loop as one unit, and you weave the weft under or over it: an 18-peg loom has 18 warp "threads". Split-loop views each strand of the warp loop as an individual unit, and you weave the weft under and over accordingly: viewed this way, an 18-peg loom has 36 warp "threads". Using the technique, you can experiment with any of the weaving structures (plain weave, twill, etc). It allows for a wonderful variety of interesting effects. Here are two to get you started.

christine's pebble weave (plain weave)

When you use the split-loop technique with a plain weave structure, you simply weave under the first arm of the warp loop and over the next arm, continuing on in the normal plain weave pattern. This gives a pebbly surface which is greatly emphasized visually if you use three colors. It's a very tight weave.

yavia's half-loopy pattern (2x2 twill), plus put a ring on it!

Yavia's Half-loopy Pattern
Row 1: under 1/over 2/under 2
Row 2: over 1/under 2/over 2
repeat

Peas and Carrots

1. Warp in 2 colors.

2. Weave under the first arm.

3. Weave over the next 2 arms.

4. Weave under the next 2 arms.

5. Continue weaving over 2/under 2...

6. ...until the end of the row.

7. Weave over the first arm, and under the next 2 arms.

8. Weave over the next 2 arms, and continue under 2/over 2 until the end of the row.

9. Repeat these 2-row steps...

10. ...you are done.

11. Crochet the potholder off the loom.

12. If you want, put a ring on. Bring the loop through the center of the ring from below.

13. Stretch the loop over the ring's top and pull through.

14. ...and voilà!

Voilà again!

13

CHAPTER 2

 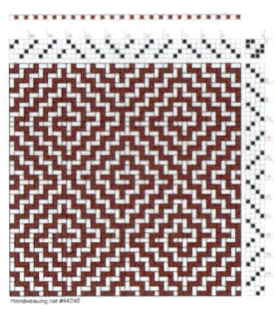  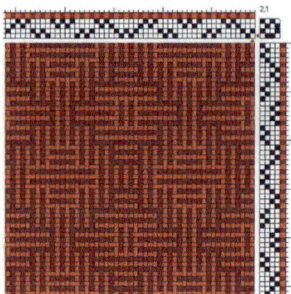

how to chart a potholder from scratch

There are several methods to chart a potholder, each dependent upon the type of weave coupled with the pattern's source: another potholder, a weaving draft, or the weaver's original idea. Plain weave, shadow weave, and twill take different charting approaches, but the beginning point, drawing the pattern that you want to chart, is the same for each, and the techniques overlap. Plain weave and basic twill are simple to chart. Converting a weaving draft to suit the potholder loom is a bit more complex, and at times is more art than science.

Weave II

Most potholder patterns are plain weave: you simply weave the weft loop over or under a warp loop, alternating weaving direction with each row. This process is so natural that we don't even think about it, let alone chart it in a potholder pattern.

So let's think about it. Plain weave is uniform, repetitious, and balanced. The pattern comes entirely from the weaver's choice of warp and weft colors, and their placement on the loom, and not at all from varying the weave structure. The weaver is bound by, and must take into account, the consistently alternating interlacing of the loops. In communicating a potholder pattern, we can write out the warp/weft sequences or we can chart them visually. For example, the chart above left is immediately understandable at a glance. It's Weave II, taken from Harrisville Design's Potholder Wizard, but more universally is the Log Cabin sequence ABABA/ABABA.

(You can generate any Log Cabin by writing a sequence of two colors, repeating the sequence reversed, and repeating the whole for the width of your loom. The pattern here is for the 18-peg loom so is *almost* repeated twice: the last 2 colors in the second repetition are missing. To weave in Log Cabin, the weft sequence is the same as the warp.)

The plain weave pattern Weave II example is the most common kind of potholder chart. In it, Harrisville Designs assumes that the weaver will know that they are to weave plain weave, and that they will begin at the lower right corner by weaving "under". (Thought experiment: what happens if they begin by weaving 'over'?). It's assumed that the weaver knows that the color dots at the top and bottom represent the warp colors and sequence, and those on the sides represent the weft colors and sequence. And Harrisville Designs is correct: we know this.

The chart to the right doesn't assume: it specifies the direction of each pick, over or under. The use of "—" for over and "|" for under mimics the way the weft looks in the fabric. Take a look at your potholder! You could, alternatively, use "o" for over and "u" for under. A method of specific charting is necessary for any potholder beyond plain weave or basic twill.

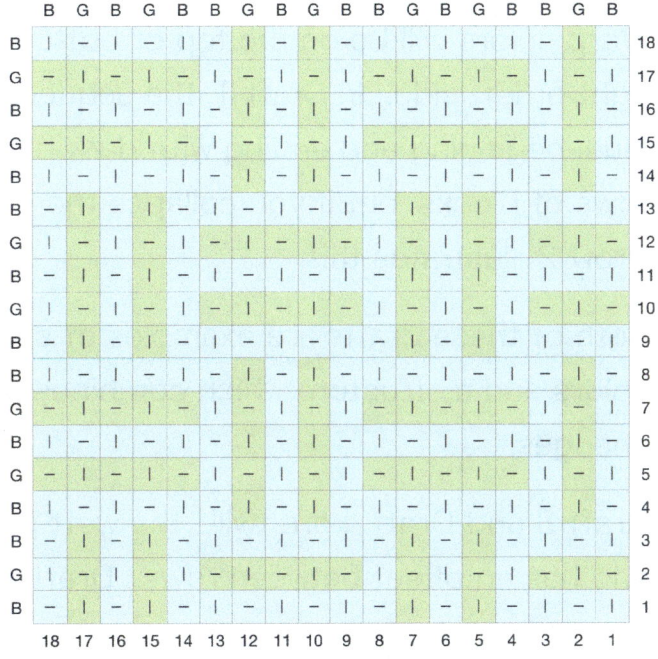

There isn't a huge catalog of potholder patterns, but there are close to 70,000 weaving drafts on handweaving.net. We could convert one of these drafts, reverse engineer any potholder, or design our own. There are different ways to do these three, but each begins with the same step: transferring the pattern to graph paper, or, if using an electronic device, a table or spreadsheet.

Draft 1: shadow weave

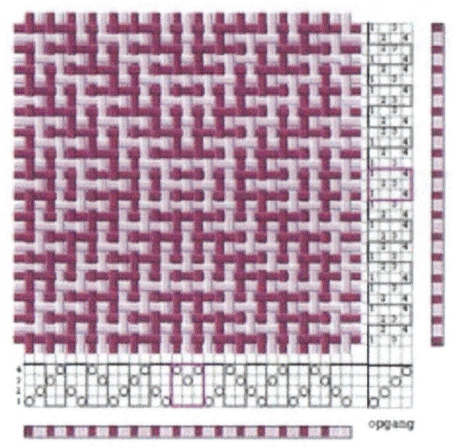

Draft 2: shadow weave

Draft 1 is a typical weaving draft. The top and sides give the threading and the treadling; the intersecting square in the upper left corner is the tie-up. If you are lucky, the weaving structure will be drawn in the draft (as in Draft 2), and your work will be only to copy the pattern of over-and-under picks, but most will look flat, as if drawn on graph paper, like Draft 1. In this most common case, the challenge is to chart the weaving structure by using the pattern and the sequence of warp and weft colors.

Warp colors will be on the top or bottom of the weaving draft. Weft will be on the right or left side. In Draft 1, the sequence of both warp and weft is dark blue/light blue, beginning and ending with dark blue. The colors move up and down the 4 rows of blocks, but if you collapse them onto one row, you'd get the sequence. Draft 2 illustrates this.

Both of these drafts are examples of shadow weave, with alternating warp and weft colors and a structure which combines plain weave with a twill-step at pattern changes.

Draft 3 and Draft 4 are twill: the weft passes over or under one or more weft loops, and has an offset between rows. Draft 3 is a basic twill: warp is one color and weft another, while Draft 4 has, like shadow weave, alternating warp and weft colors. This difference is significant when charting. The charting steps 1-3 don't apply to basic twill or plain weave: these are discussed at the chapter's end.

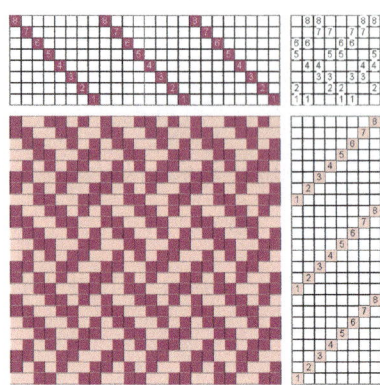

Draft 3: basic twill

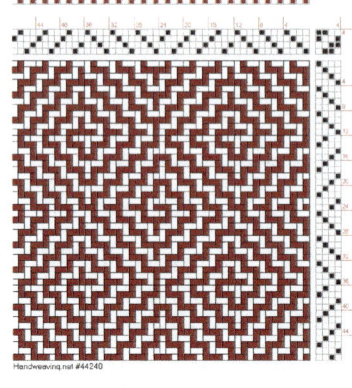

Draft 4: twill

STEP 0 The first goal is to transfer the pattern from the draft to graph paper or, if using your laptop, tablet, or computer, into a table. Print out the draft, choose the block that fits your loom, and clearly mark it off.

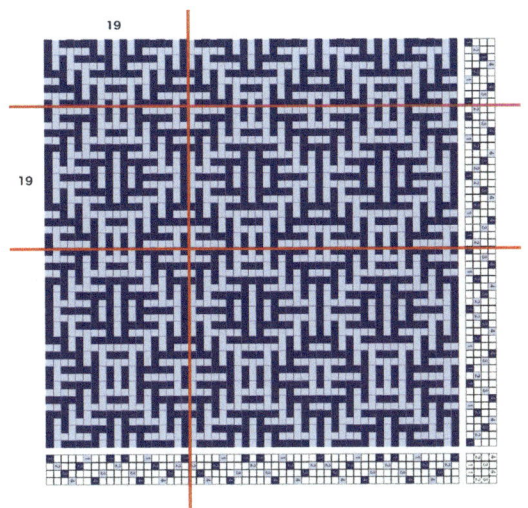

Because the pattern is symmetrical around one central point, and I have a nice 19-peg loom made for me by CottageLoomsDesigns on Etsy, I've marked off a 19x19 block. To fit the standard 18-peg loom, just drop a row and column.

Tip: For those of you with both 18 and 27-peg looms, chart the 27-peg first — it's easier to then size down for the smaller loom.

Transfer the pattern to a grid: graph paper and a pencil works perfectly. Alternatively, use a table or Excel spreadsheet. I mark the center square with an asterisk, then fill in the pattern. The warp and weft colors will be blue and white, so I've marked those at the top and side, referring to the draft to make sure the sequence begins and ends correctly.

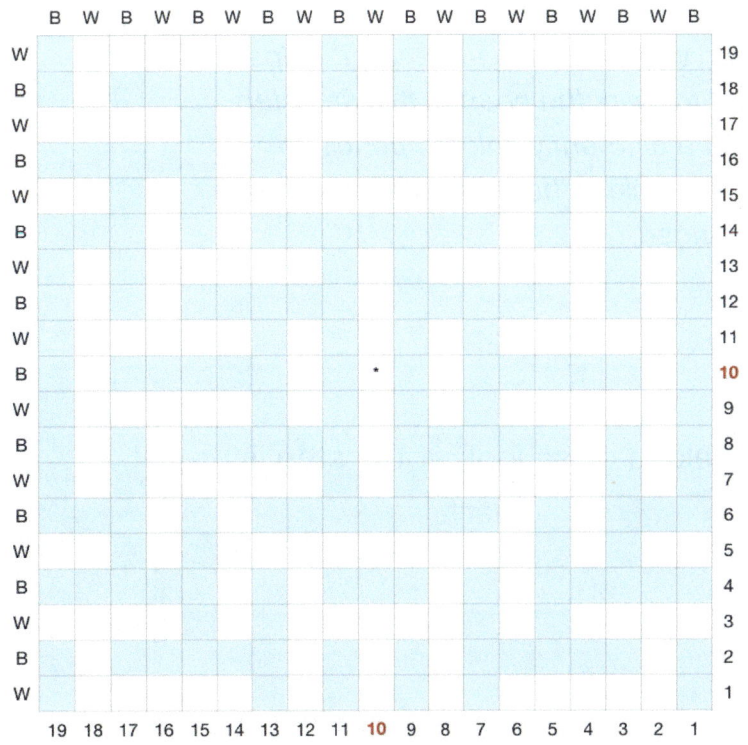

STEP 1 Next, begin to chart the weaving structure. Look at the upper left side of the table below: in order to make the pattern, the white weft loop **must** go under the first blue warp loop, and over the next two blue ones. In the same way, the blue weft **must** go under the first white warp loop and over the next two white warp loops. These picks are fixed, and can't change.

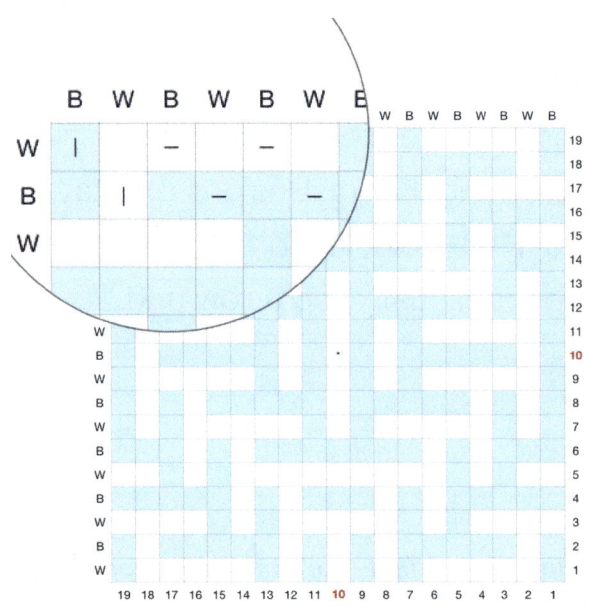

At this point, the direction of the weave under or over those warp loops which are the same color as the weft isn't considered, because the pattern color at those picks remains the same either way.

Tip: when working in pencil, it helps at first to mark the chart in this first step with a differently colored pencil, to make it clear that this notation can't be changed.

Take a close look at the step 1 chart.

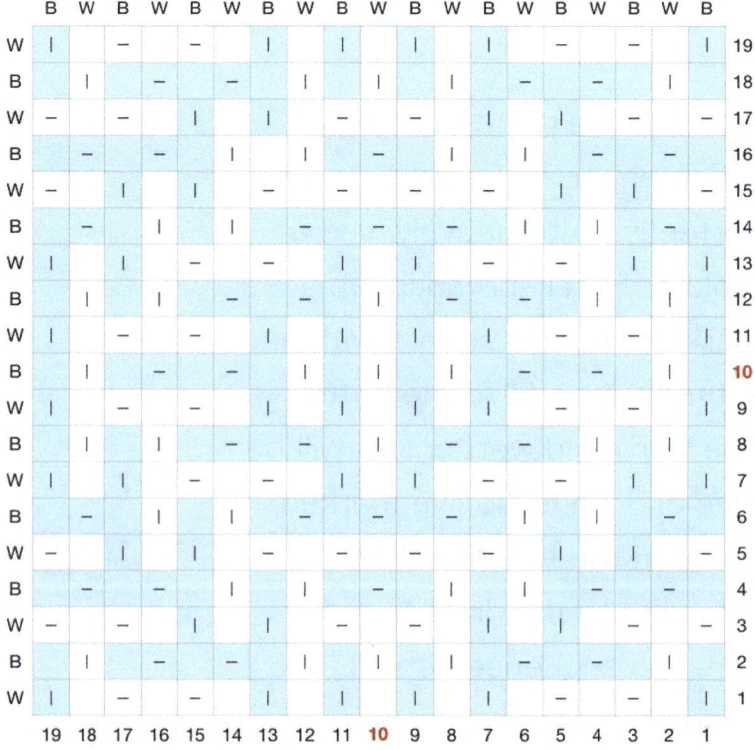

Step 1 notation is filled in.

STEP 2 Next, go through and look at each empty square and the pick notation surrounding it. If there are 3 or 4 "under" marks (|) then place an "over" (—) in the square. If there are 3 or 4 "over" marks, place an "under" in the square. Note that corners are the exception! Corners and edges can, if you want, wait to be filled in until the end. Depending on the pattern, this can be desirable, as it gives you more flexibility.

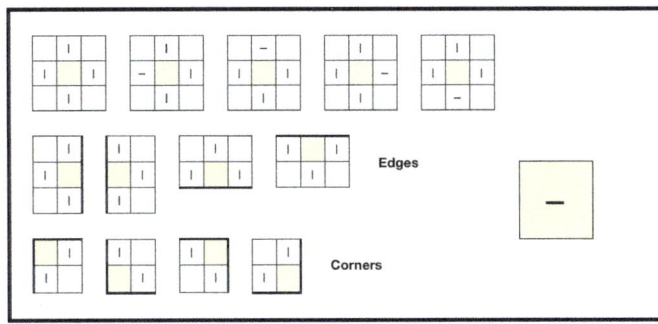

How to place step 2 "over" notation.

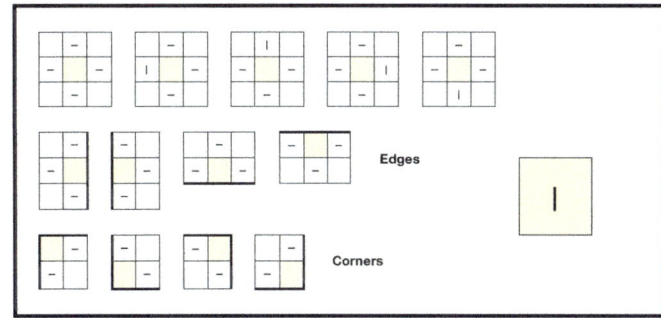

How to place step 2 "under" notation.

In Figure 1, the top row, 4th square from the left is surrounded to each side and the bottom by "—" notation. We place an "|" there (Figure 2). Similarly, in the 2nd row, 3rd square from the left, we place an "|", as it's surrounded on 3 sides by "—" notation.

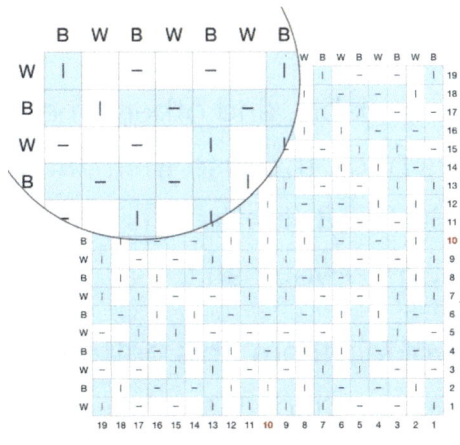

Figure 1

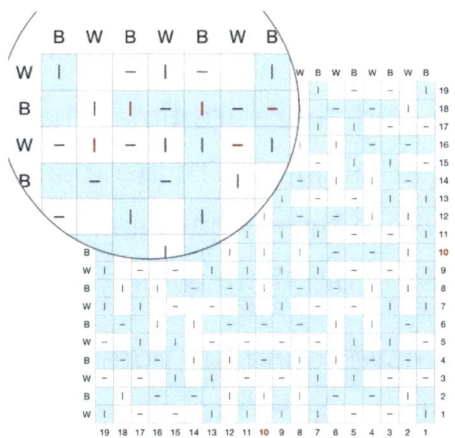

Figure 2

19

STEP 3 For the last few squares, the goal is to produce as balanced and tight a weave as possible. To do this, avoid 3 "under" (|) or "over" (—) floats in a row either horizontally or vertically. These potential long overshots are easy to spot. Three areas are circled in Figure 3, and Figure 4 shows the filled in notation. There are a few more places where potential 3-floats exist: see if you can find them.

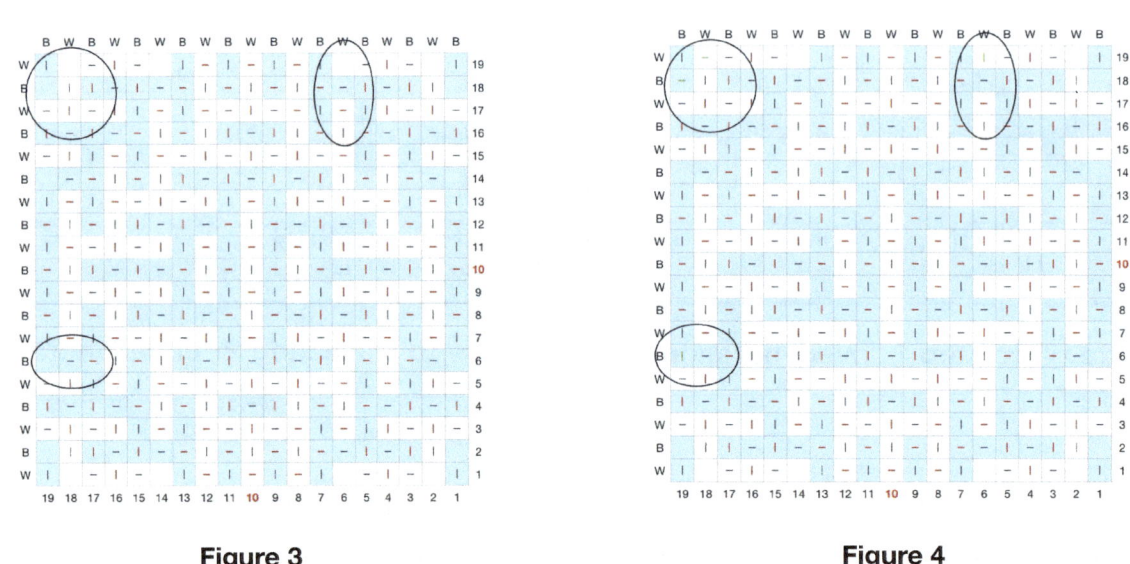

Figure 3   Figure 4

In general, 3-floats should be avoided in potholder charting. Because the loop floats over (or under) 3 others, it's not as stabilized by the weaving interlace, so the finished potholder will draw in more at that point, possibly distorting the fabric. They're most problematic on an edge, and it's best to avoid them there.

This being said, there are times that a 3-float is unavoidable, and other times when it adds to the design. There are many patterns in this book that use them, and patterns where three-floats appear at the edges. So the 3-float rule is rather ambiguous: avoid them when you can, but don't worry if you can't.

When you have found the potential 3-floats, and avoided them, this pattern has no more empty squares, Step 3 is finished, you're done charting. It's more often, though, not this easy. Next are more examples of what you might encounter, and how to chart them, if after Step 3 you are still left with blank squares.

HINT FOR SYMMETRICAL PATTERNS: Our example pattern is symmetrical along both axes: row 1 is the same as row 19; row 2 is the same as row 18; row 3 is the same as row 17; and on in the same way up to row 9 and row 11. Each row is also symmetrical within itself: row 1, column 1 is the same as row 1, column 19; row 1, column 2 is the same as row 1, column 18; and on until row 1, column 9 = row 1, column 11. If there were blank squares at any position, you'd look at the corresponding square in its row and use the same notation. This hint is for symmetrical patterns only, and usually is needed only if you've missed a square.

HINT FOR DIAGONALS: Most often there are blank squares along several different diagonals. With these, you have more choice, as it generally doesn't matter how you fill them in. Pick a method (all "under" picks or all "over" picks, for example), and be both mindful of the surrounding squares — your first consideration will be avoiding any float of 3 over or under — and as consistent as the surrounding squares allow.

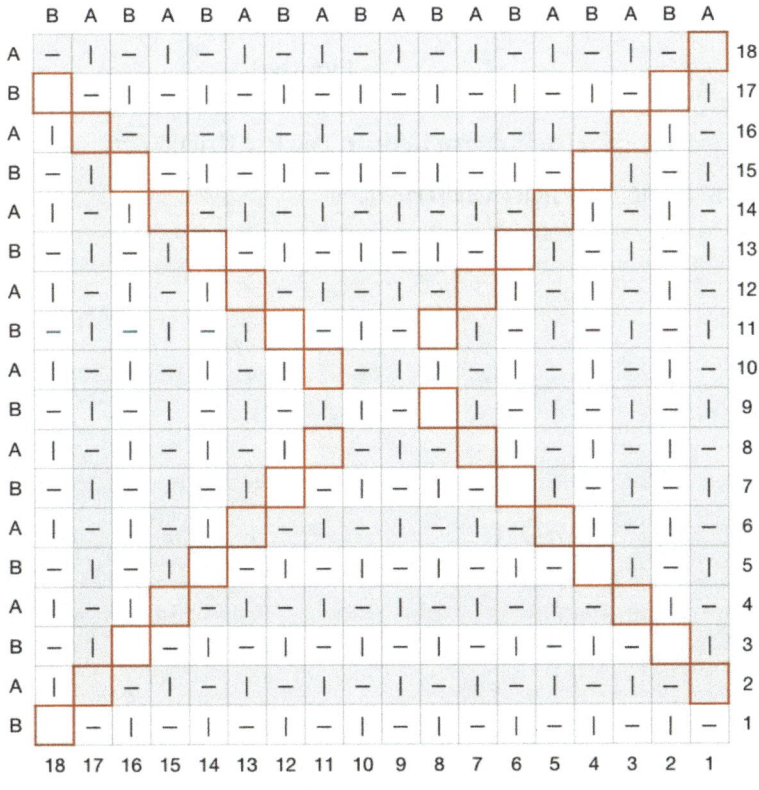

This is Mary Clarke's Straight-Edged Spiral — a simple example of squares on diagonal runs. (The pattern can be found in this book.)

Note that blank squares are surrounded by 2 under ("|") and 2 over ("—") notation.

STACKED PAIRS: If you fill Straight-Edged Spiral's diagonals with all over (—) notation, you get the chart in Figure 5. Stacked pairs of under (|) picks and over (—) picks are outlined in red. These don't happen to adversely affect the tightness of the weave, and can be used as design elements. But, if you wanted, you could reduce the stack, as in Figure 6. Try it both ways, see how the weave looks, and decide.

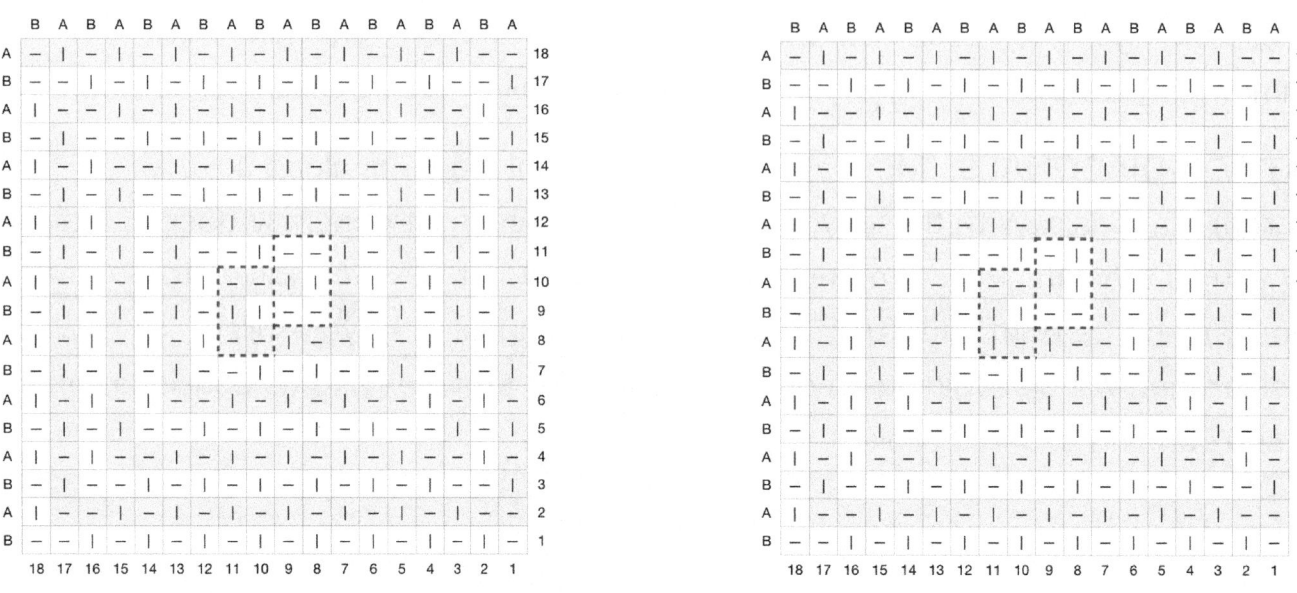

Figure 5   **Figure 6**

Below is Mary's Fillet pattern. Stacked pairs of under and over picks flank either side of the central column, and form a strong design element.

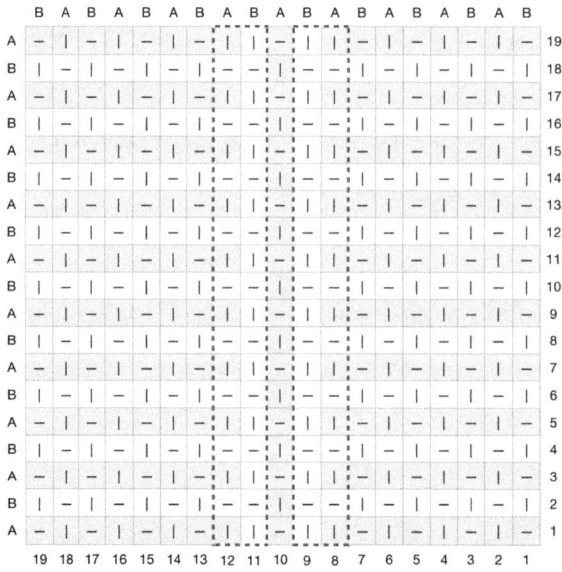

SOMETIMES YOU MUST CHANGE THE PATTERN, OR NOT: Figure 7 is an early version of a two-pattern mashup that I have been playing with. Look at the squares within the red box: two opposing under picks and two opposing over picks. Both an under and an over in the center square will result in a 3-float. This configuration is a charting nemesis. The choices are to re-design the pattern, or accept the 3-floats. My advice: experiment. Try the floats and see what happens with the final structure. More often than not the design will work.

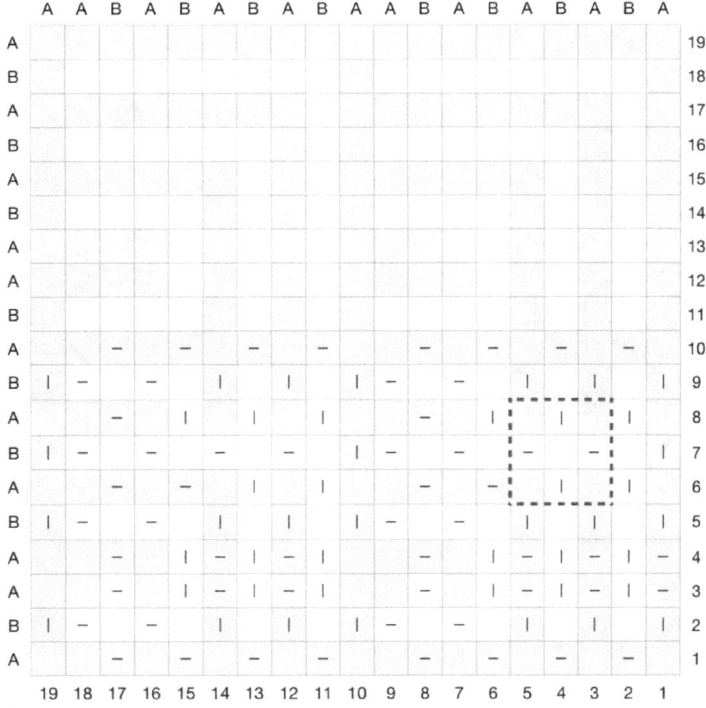

Figure 7

At this point I want to add that not all weaving drafts are suited to a potholder loom conversion. There'll be drafts you think will surely work, but they won't. Just never lose your sense of adventure, and keep trying — there are amazing patterns out there!

The charting steps 1-3 so far discussed apply to all weaves (as far as I know) but plain weave and basic twill. These two weaving structures are easy to chart.

CHARTING BASIC TWILL: Basic twill is simple to chart. In fact, no chart is needed. Look at the draft below: the warp is all green, the weft white. So, everywhere the green warp shows, the weft loop is woven under the warp loop. Everywhere the white weft shows, the weft loop is woven over the warp loop. So, looking at the magnifier in Figure 9, the weft loop on the first row would be woven: over 2, under 1, over 2, under 1, over 2....and so on.

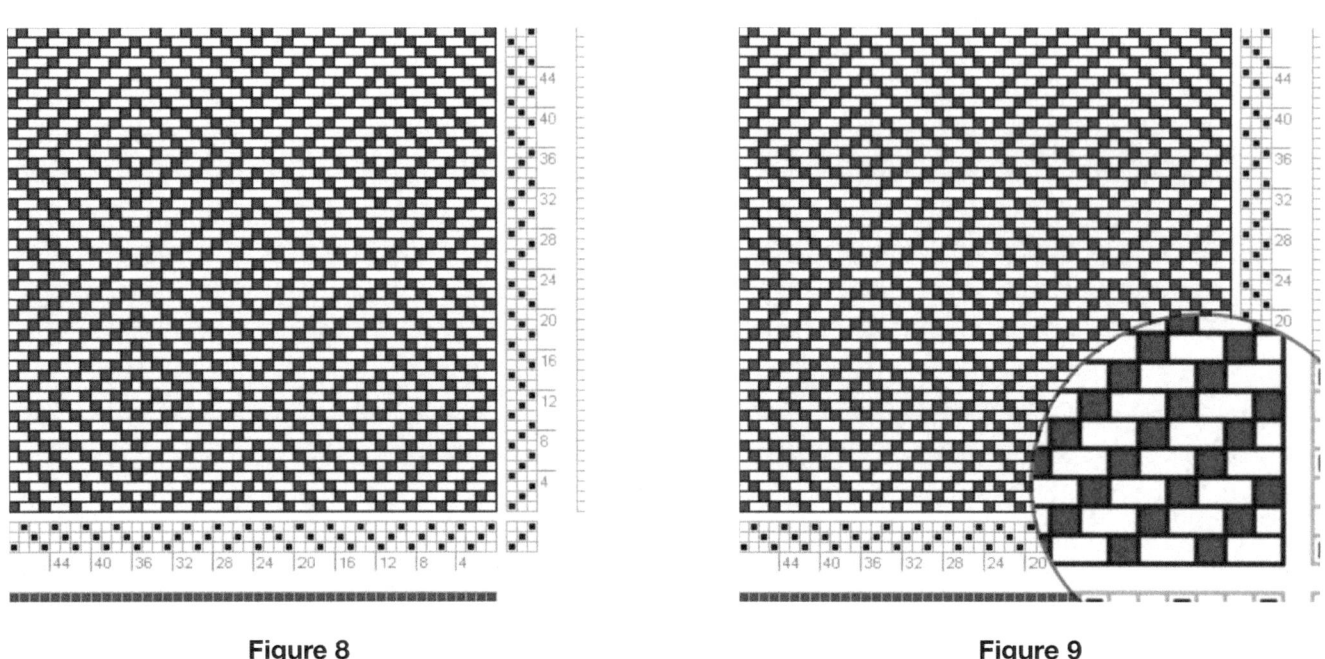

Figure 8   **Figure 9**

The second row would be woven: over 1, under 1, over 2, under 1, over 2, under 1....and so on. After Step 0, there is really nothing more to do but weave. Try it with Figure 8. (Note the 3-floats in this pattern.)

CHARTING PLAIN WEAVE: Plain weave is also simple. To reverse engineer any existing plain weave potholder (actually any potholder!) just examine the warp and weft loops and transcribe their direction to your chart, noting the beginning weave direction at the bottom right. If not plain weave, use over-and-under notation throughout. Some people do this directly onto the loom, weaving as they go, and photograph the loom before crocheting the potholder off. The photo serves as your chart.

SUMMARY

For all weaves except plain and basic twill

Step 0: Transfer the pattern to paper or digital media; make sure the warp and weft colors are properly charted.

Step 1: Fill in the notation for the required picks.

Step 2: Fill in the notation around blank squares according to Step 2's placement rules.

Step 3: Fill in the remaining blank squares, avoiding 3-floats where possible.

For basic twill

Where the warp loop color shows, weave the weft loop under. Where the weft loop color shows, weave the weft loop over.

For plain weave

Transcribe the warp and weft colors, and direction of weave, to the chart by examining the weave structure.

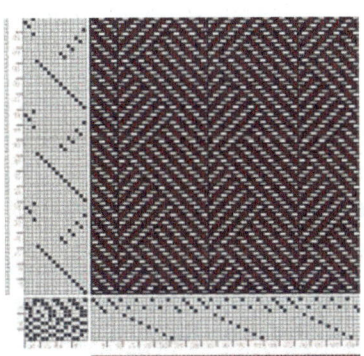 

There are so many exciting drafts on handweaving.net, Pinterest, a Google Images search. I wish you many happy hours finding them and making your unique potholder a reality.

CHAPTER 3
potholder patterns: plain weave

Plain weave (also called tabby) is a basic weaving structure in which the weft is woven over or under each warp loop, alternating with each row. This produces a flat fabric with a checkered surface, which, because of the tight interlocking of thread, is very strong. The design can't take advantage of a varying weave, so must depend on tabby's consistency coupled with the color and color sequence of warp and weft. Basket weave, where threads (in our case, loops) are bundled together and woven as one, is a form of plain weave. You could play with design using basket weave, and also thicker and thinner loops; you could play with color to create pattern.

Plain weave is the most common kind of potholder weaving, with tremendous variety and potential. Harrisville Designs has an online Potholder Wizard with which you can generate endless patterns using their color palette: it's a happy way to spend time, and you may find good strong designs serendipitously. There are many patterns on the internet, in social media groups, and in a few books. The intention in this chapter is to gather together the strongest classic tabby designs all in one place, and you may find a few surprises as well.

Fun fact: the word 'tabby' comes from a taffeta fabric of silk and cotton made in the 12th century in Attabiya, a district of Baghdad. It was called attābī, and morphed through French as 'tabis' to the English 'tabby'.

Ππ

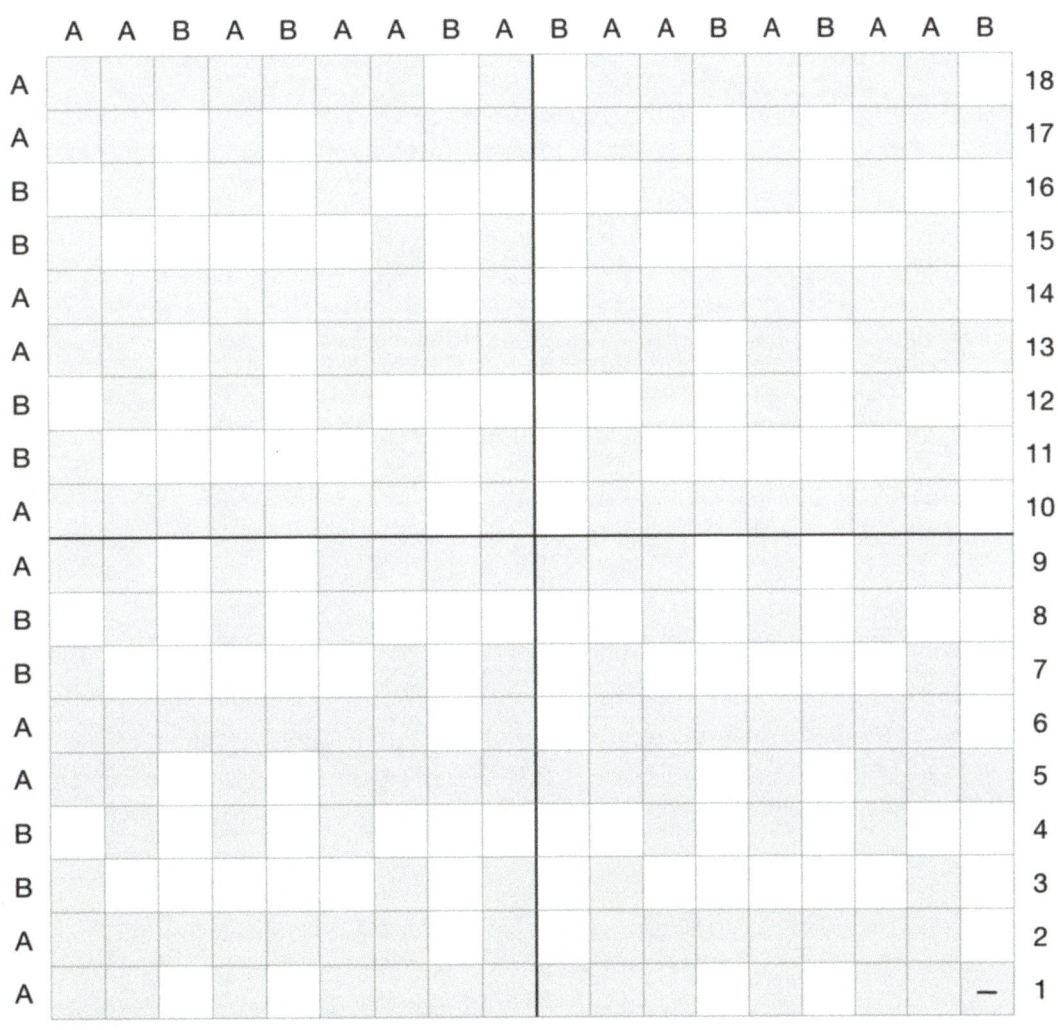

Stripes
a fundamental weaving technique

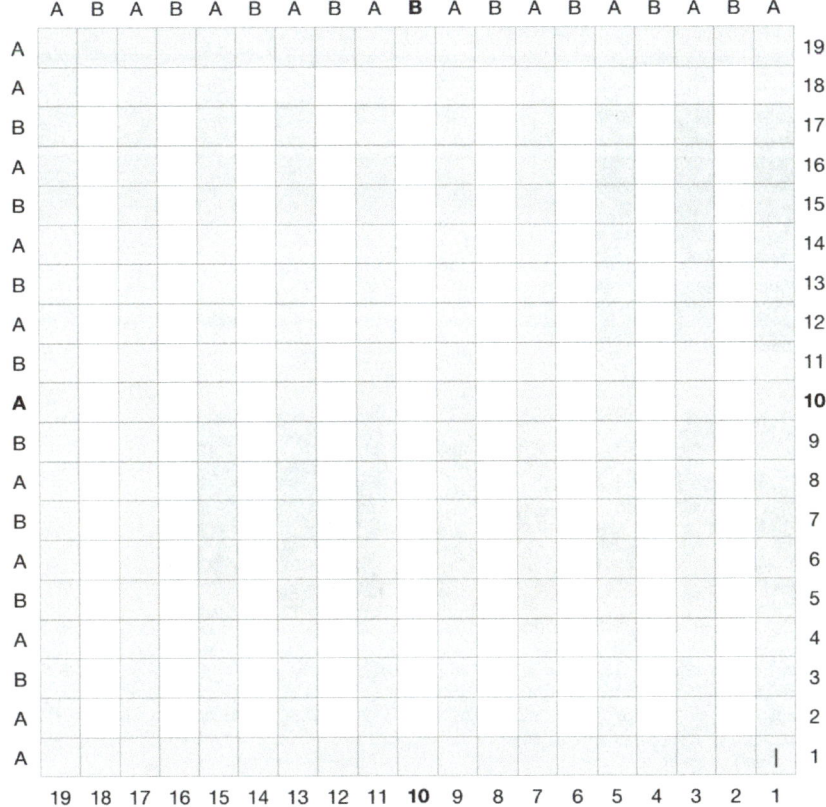

Stripes with a frame. This potholder is woven with Harrisville Turquoise and loops cut from a sock.

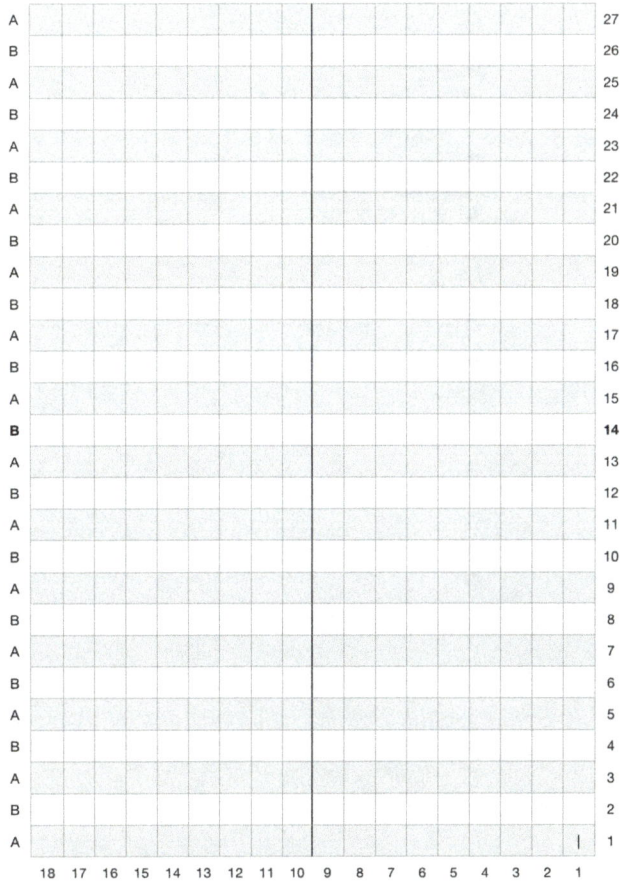

29

Kantha

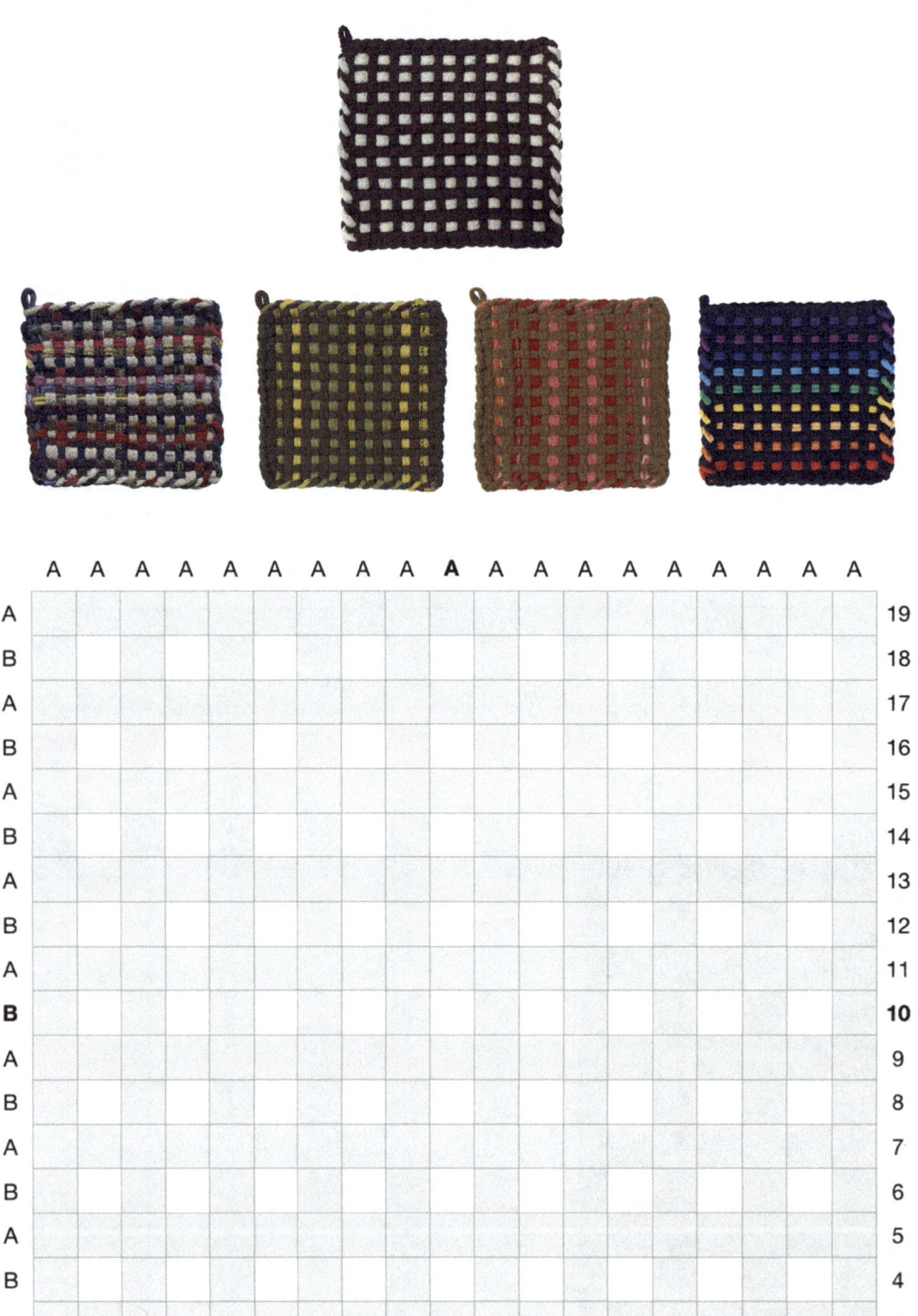

For any size loom, the warp and weft sequence is simply continued across the length and width of the loom. Here's two 27 peg examples.

A cheerful 18-peg Kantha from Michelle Spaulding in Harrisville Designs colors.
Warp White/Black across.
Weft, from bottom to top:

1. Green
2. Blue
3. Orange
4. Plum
5. Pink
6. Turquoise
7. Lime
8. Carnation
9. Yellow
10. Green
11. Blue
12. Salmon
13. Plum
14. Pink
15. Turquoise
16. Lime
17. Carnation
18. Yellow

Broken Comb

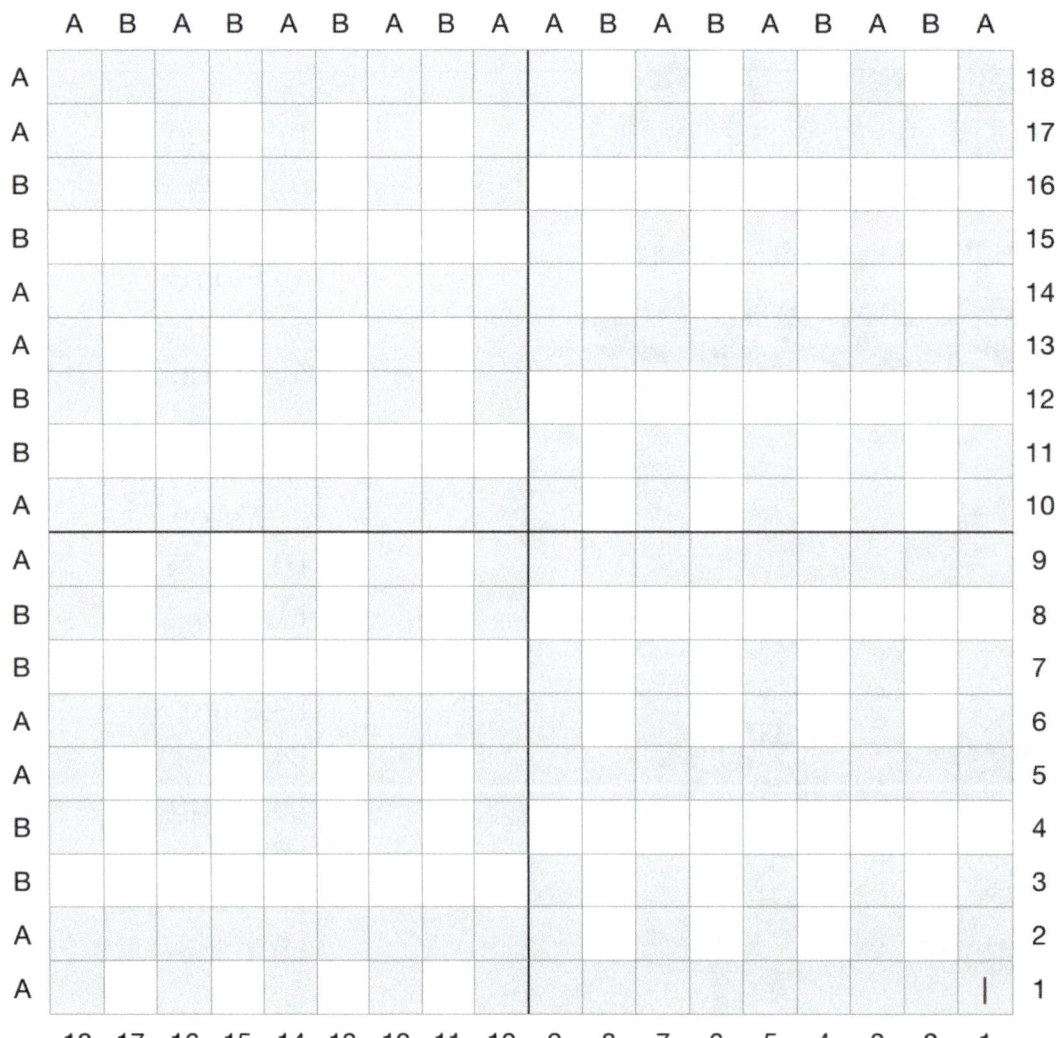

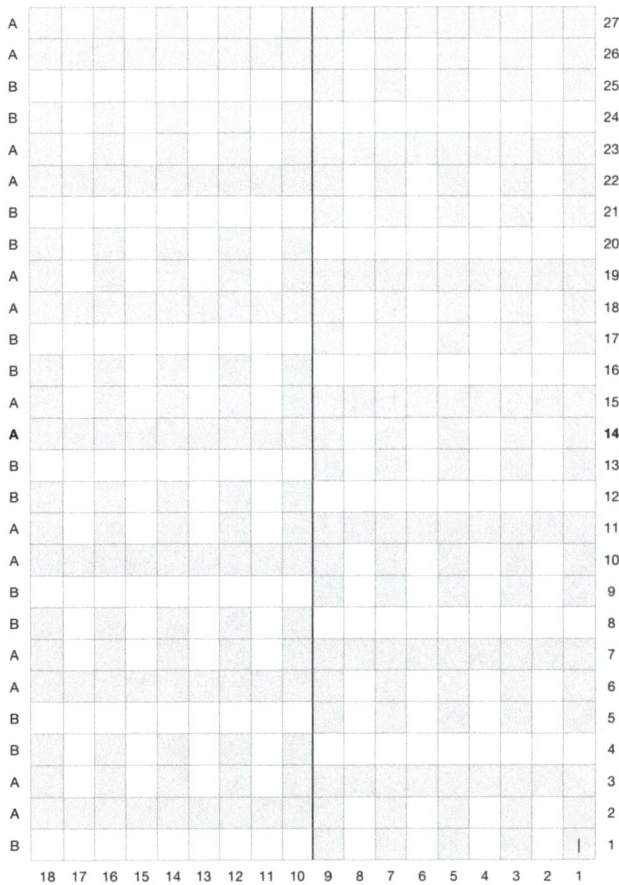

33

Broken Ladders

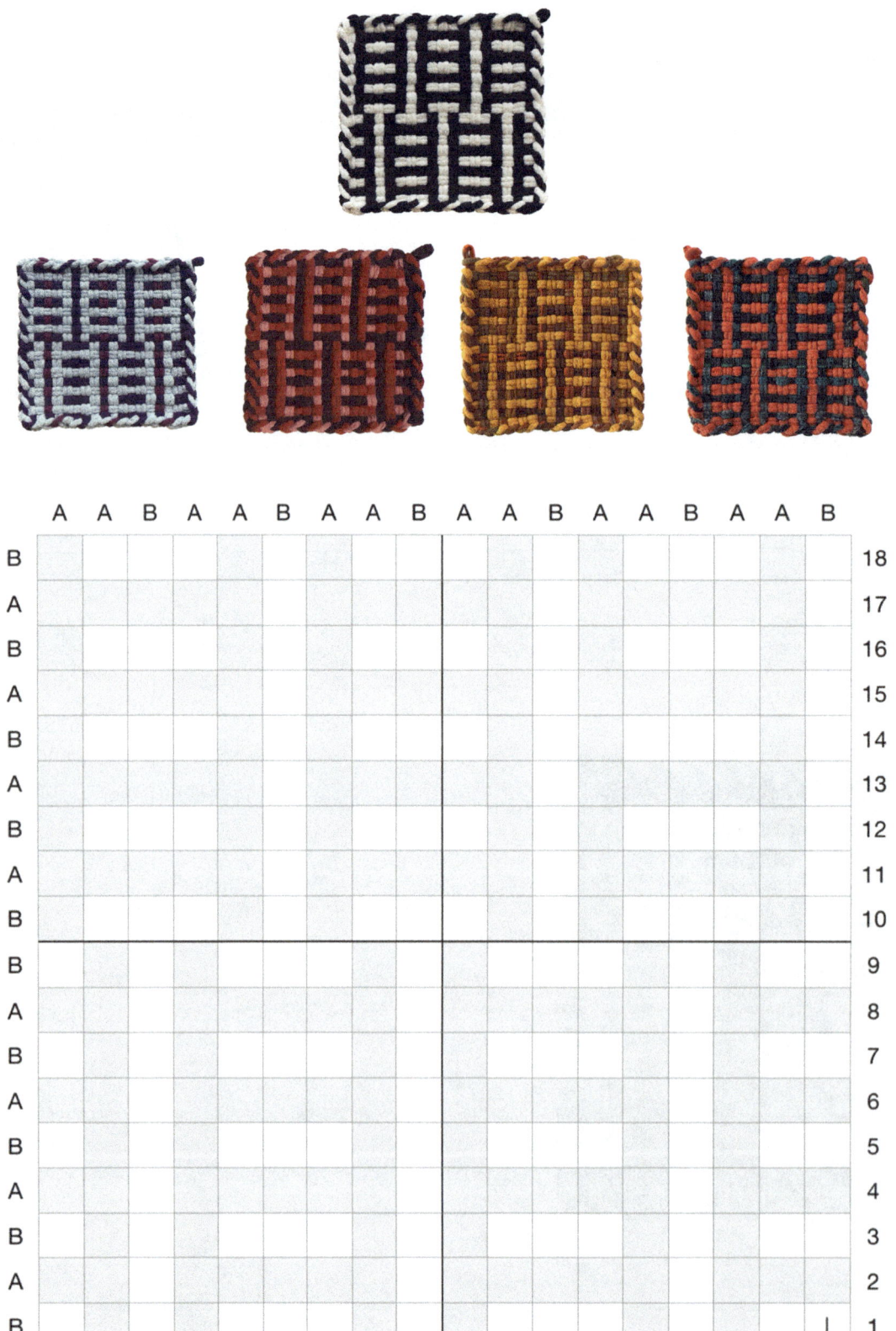

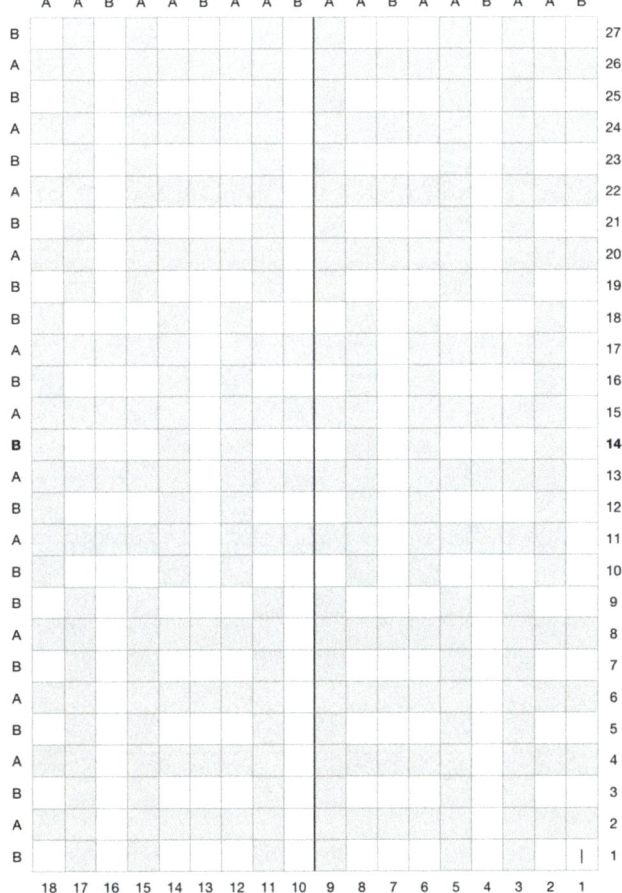

35

Comb

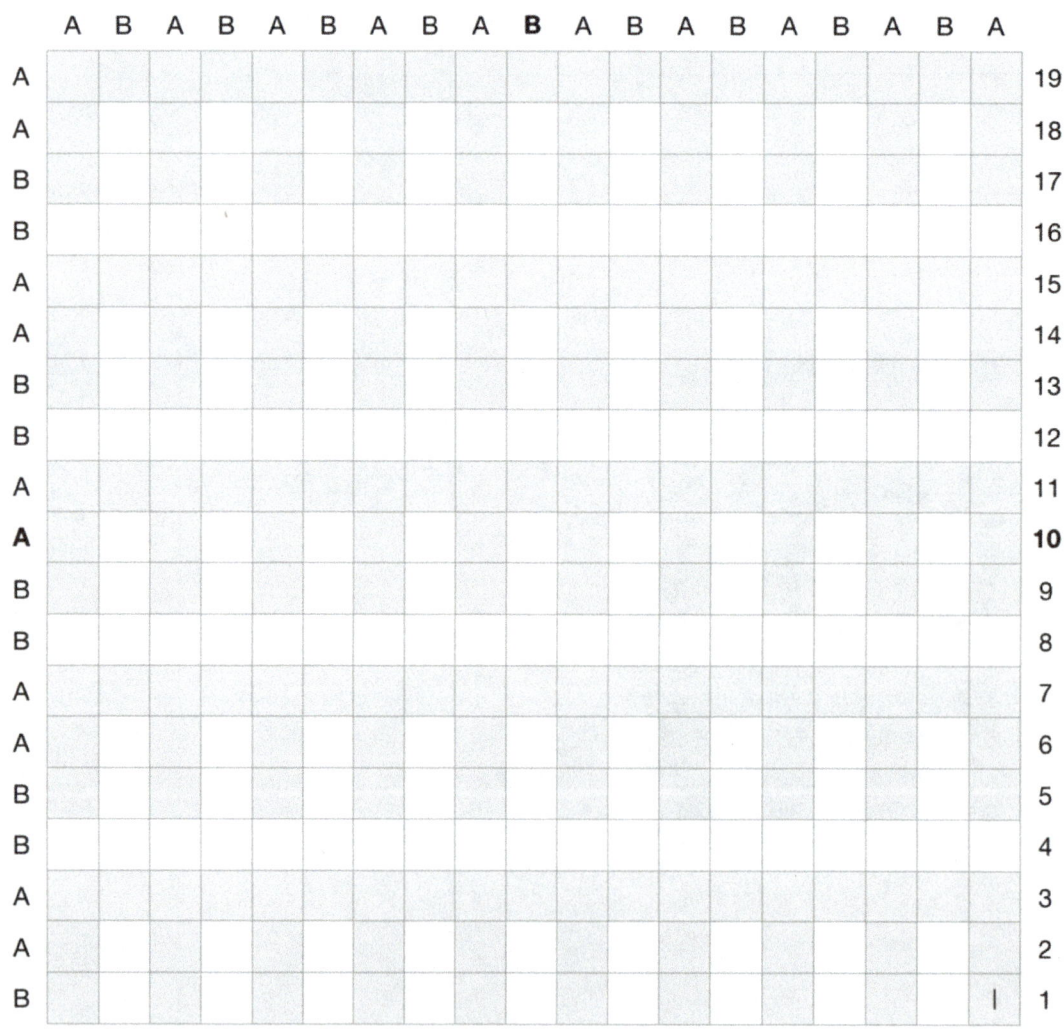

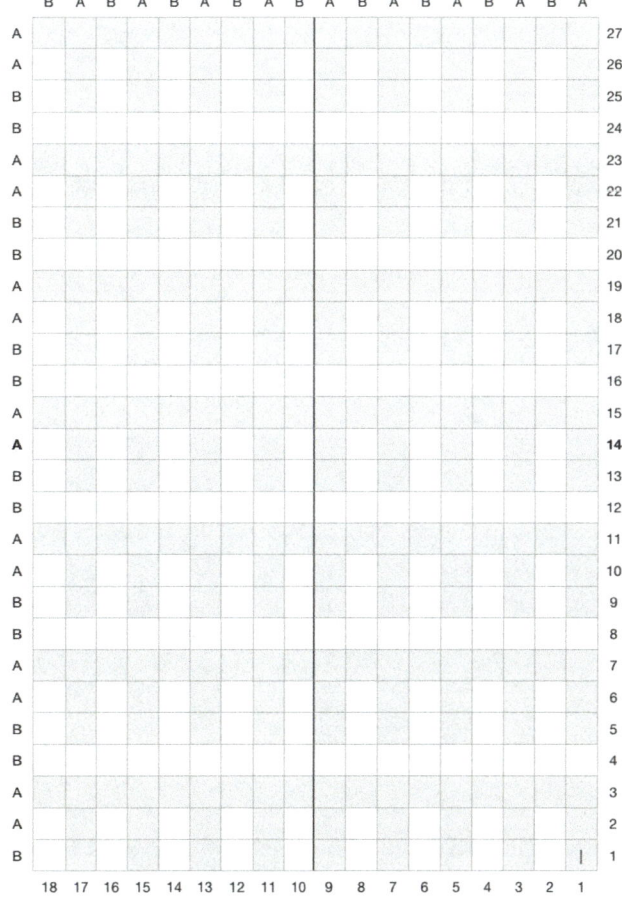

37

Comb Variation
original design, Deborah Jean Cohen

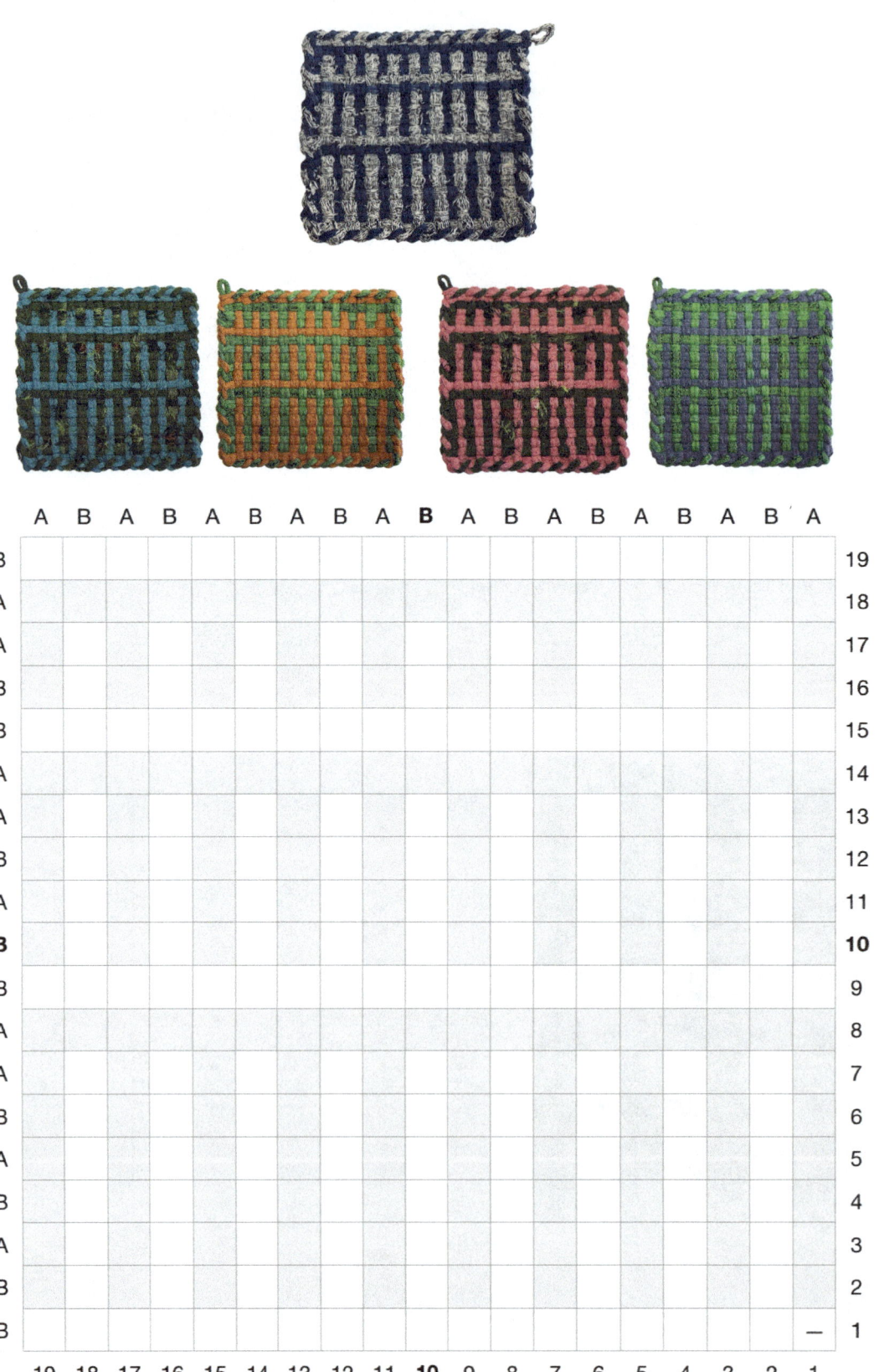

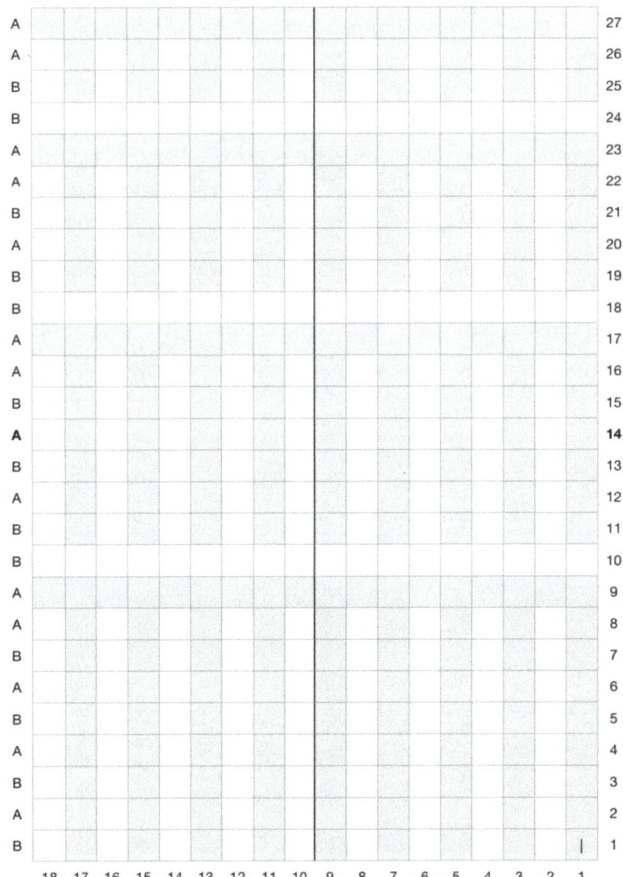

Ladders

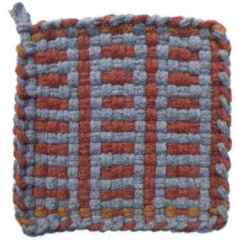

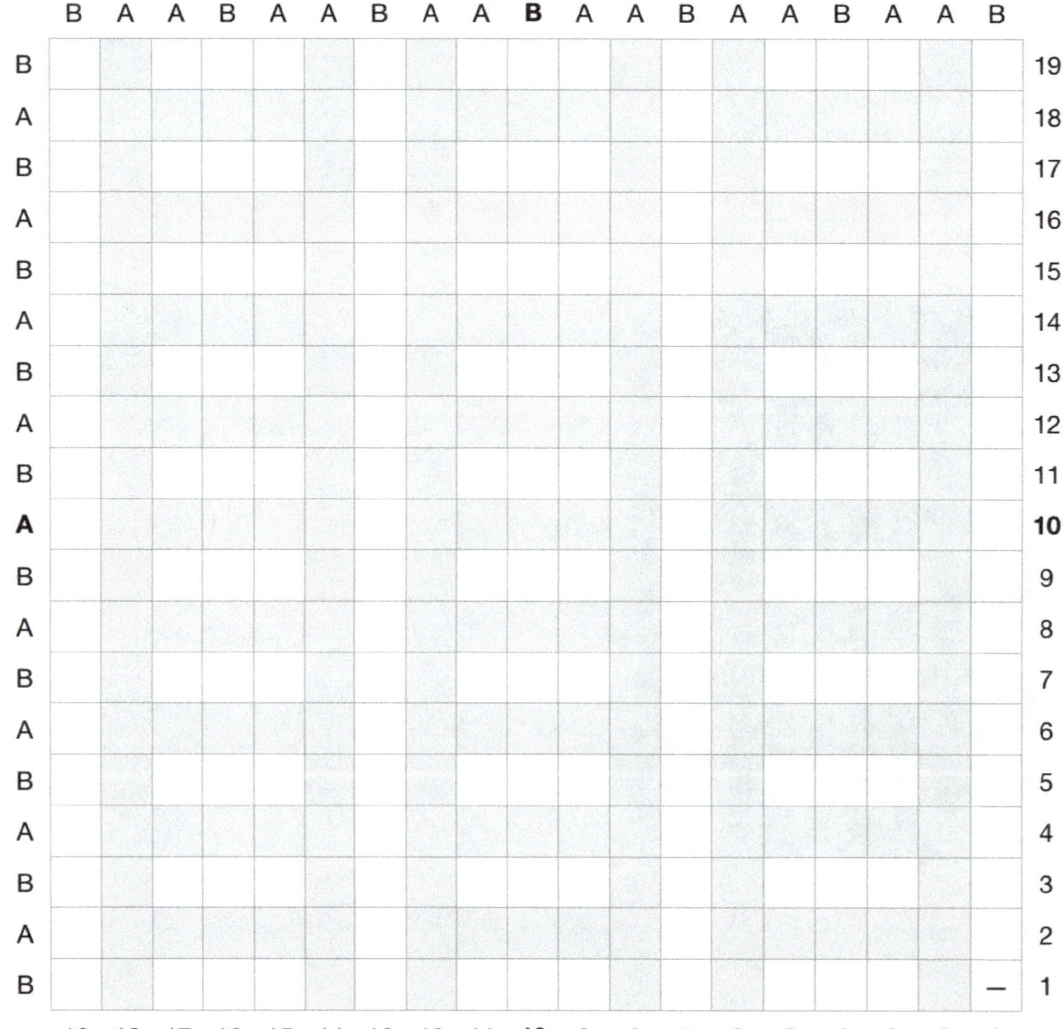

This potholder is a variation: the ladder rungs span 5 loops rather than 3. Woven on a 19 peg loom. Warp, from left top: BABA to end, ends with B. Weft, from bottom: BB AABABAA B AABABAA BB.

Mary has stealthed the ladders by substituting two similar shades (Salmon and Pink) for A, and Black and Silver for B. Using color for the ladders and a neutral for the background makes the ladders pop, at the same time that the 4 colors break up the design: delightfully interesting!

Log Cabin ABABAB

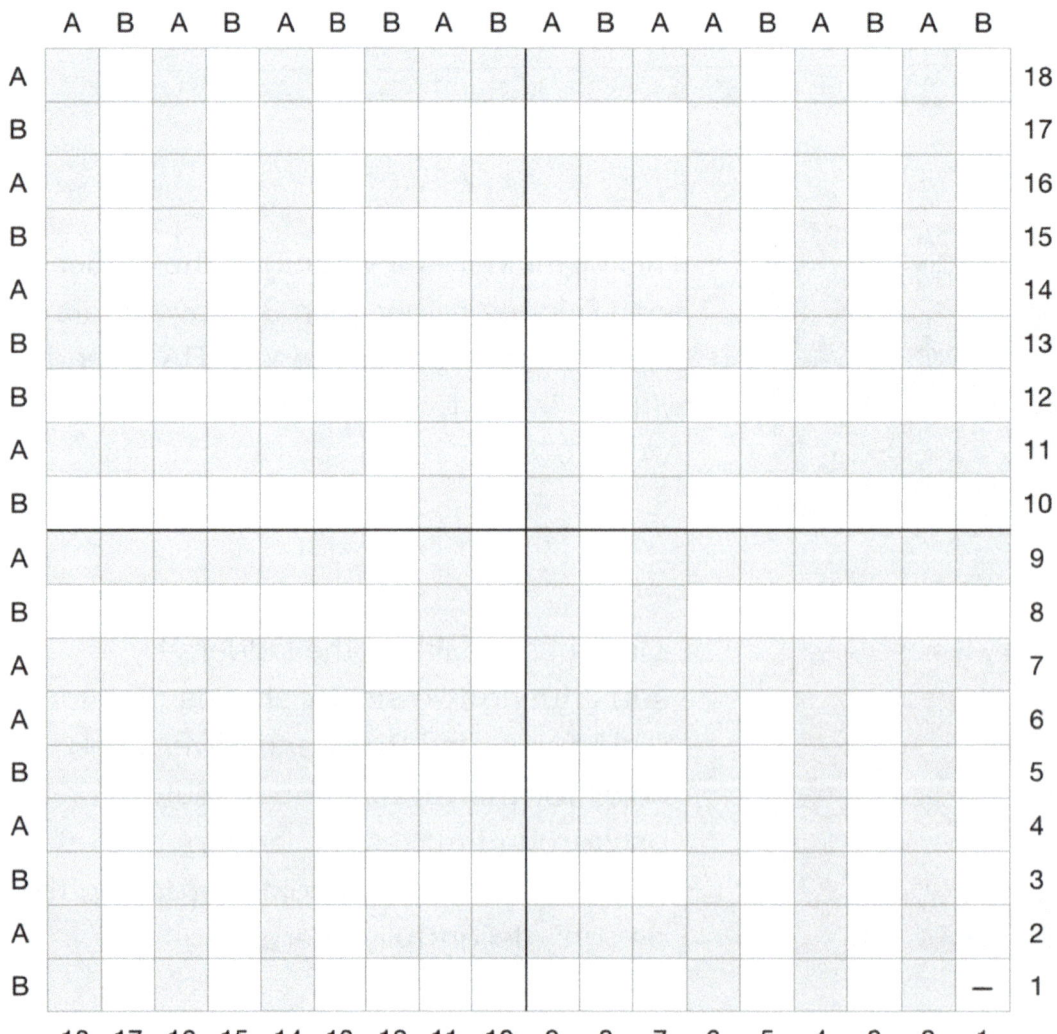

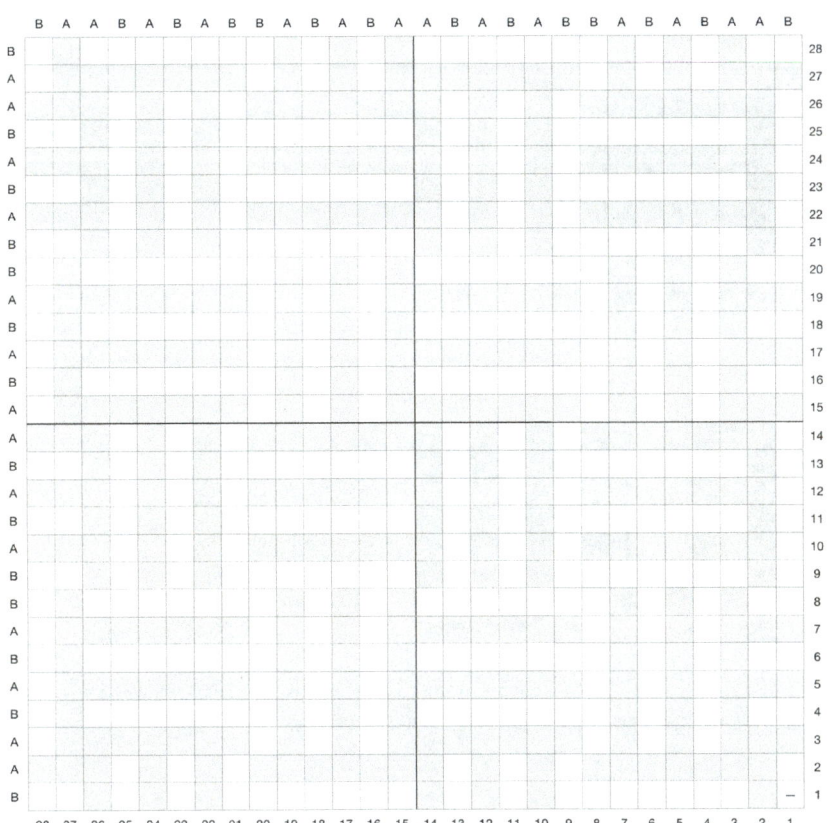

The Log Cabin Rule

Log Cabin is woven by warping a sequence of two alternating colors, repeating the sequence reversed, and repeating the whole for the width of your loom. Weft follows the warp sequence. The 28 peg chart for this pattern, ABA/ABA, is centered, so begins with the end of the sequence.

You can weave log cabin on any loom using this rule.

Catherine Wheels

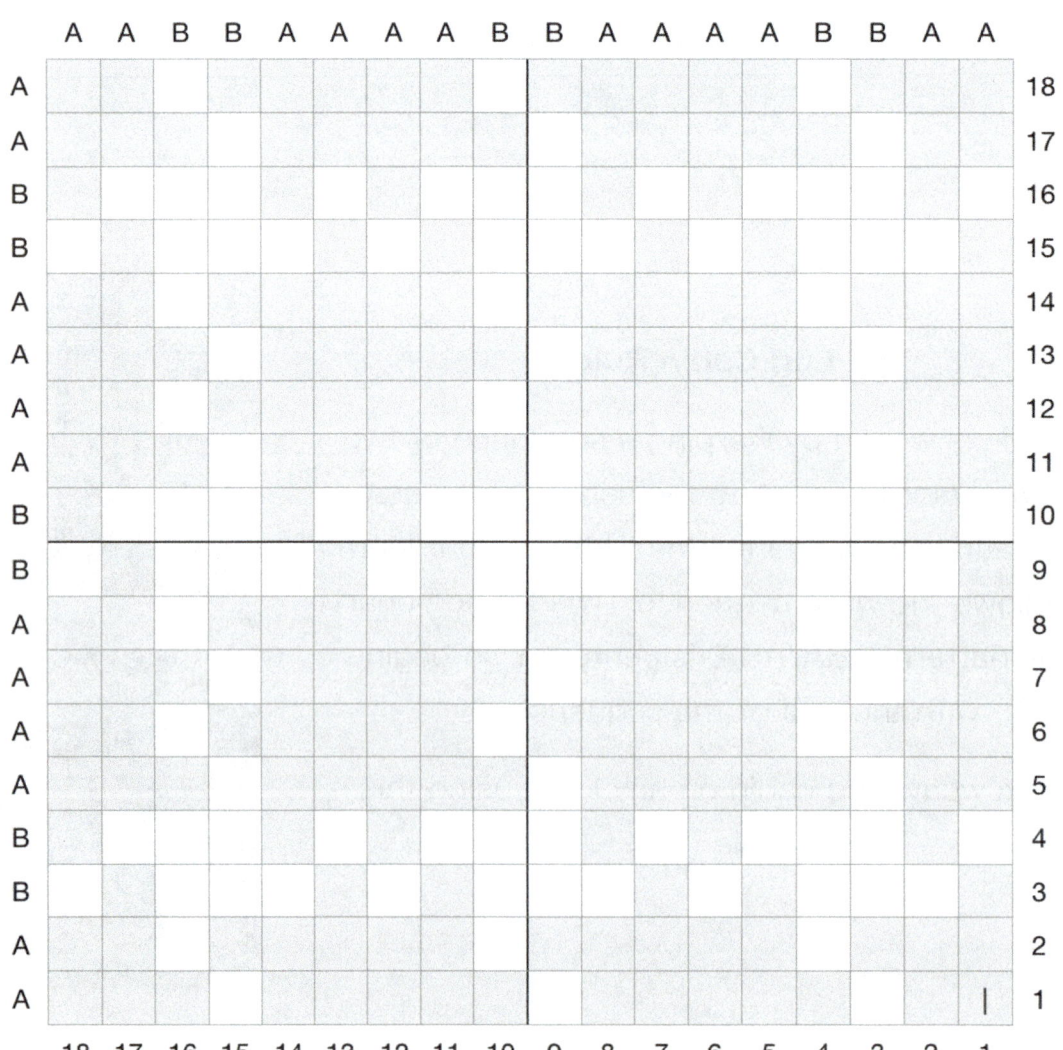

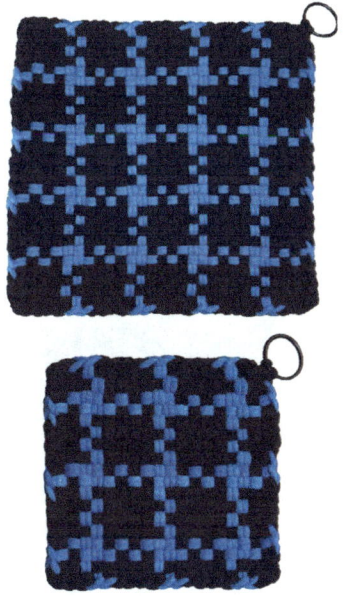

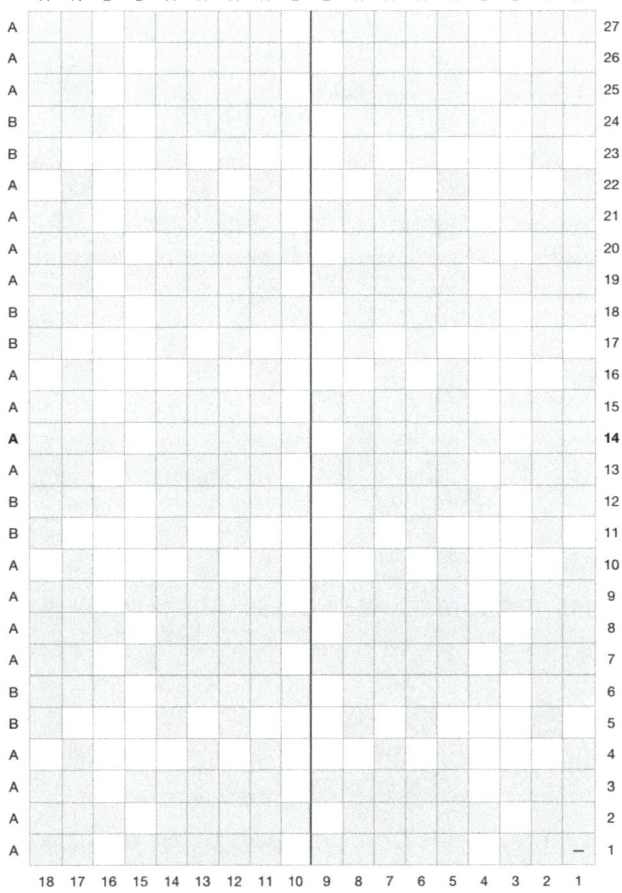

Confetti
Log Cabin BAB/BAB

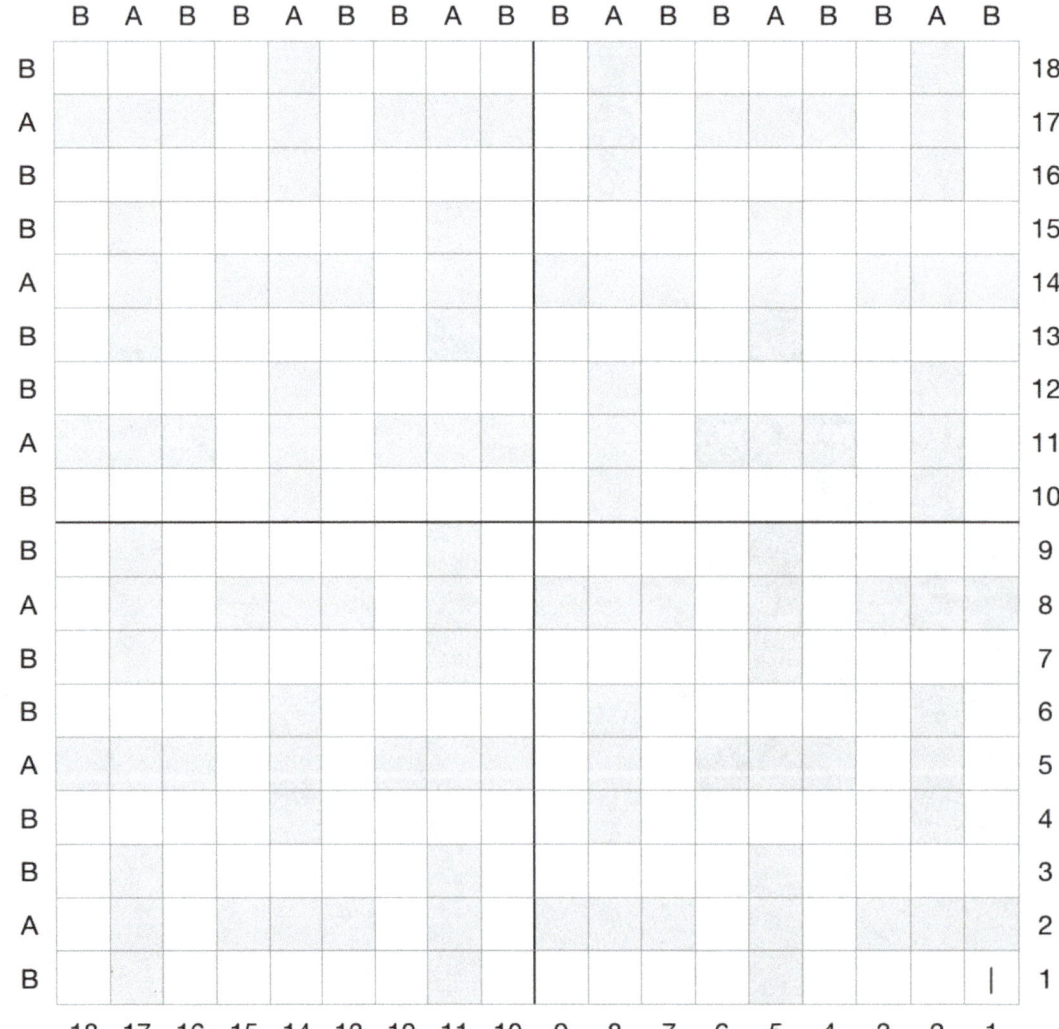

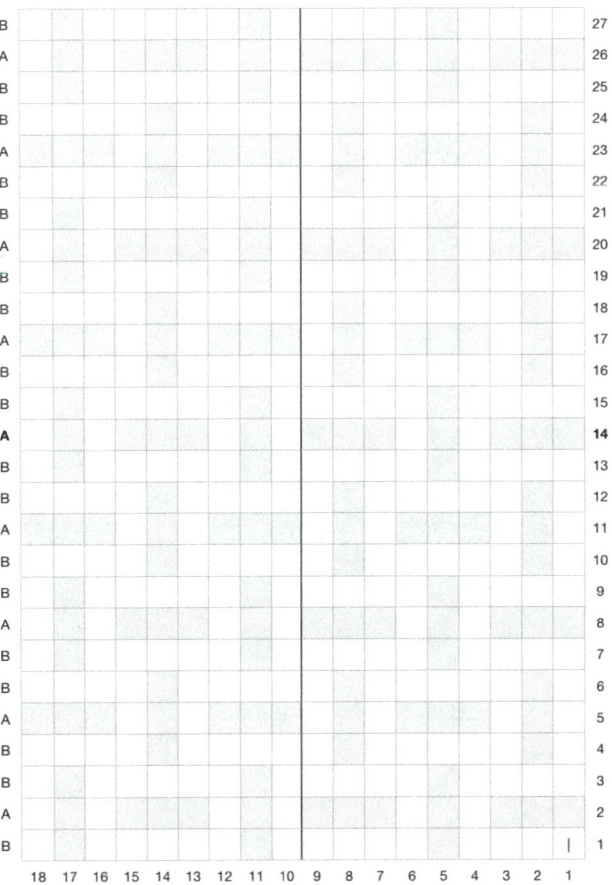

Film Strips

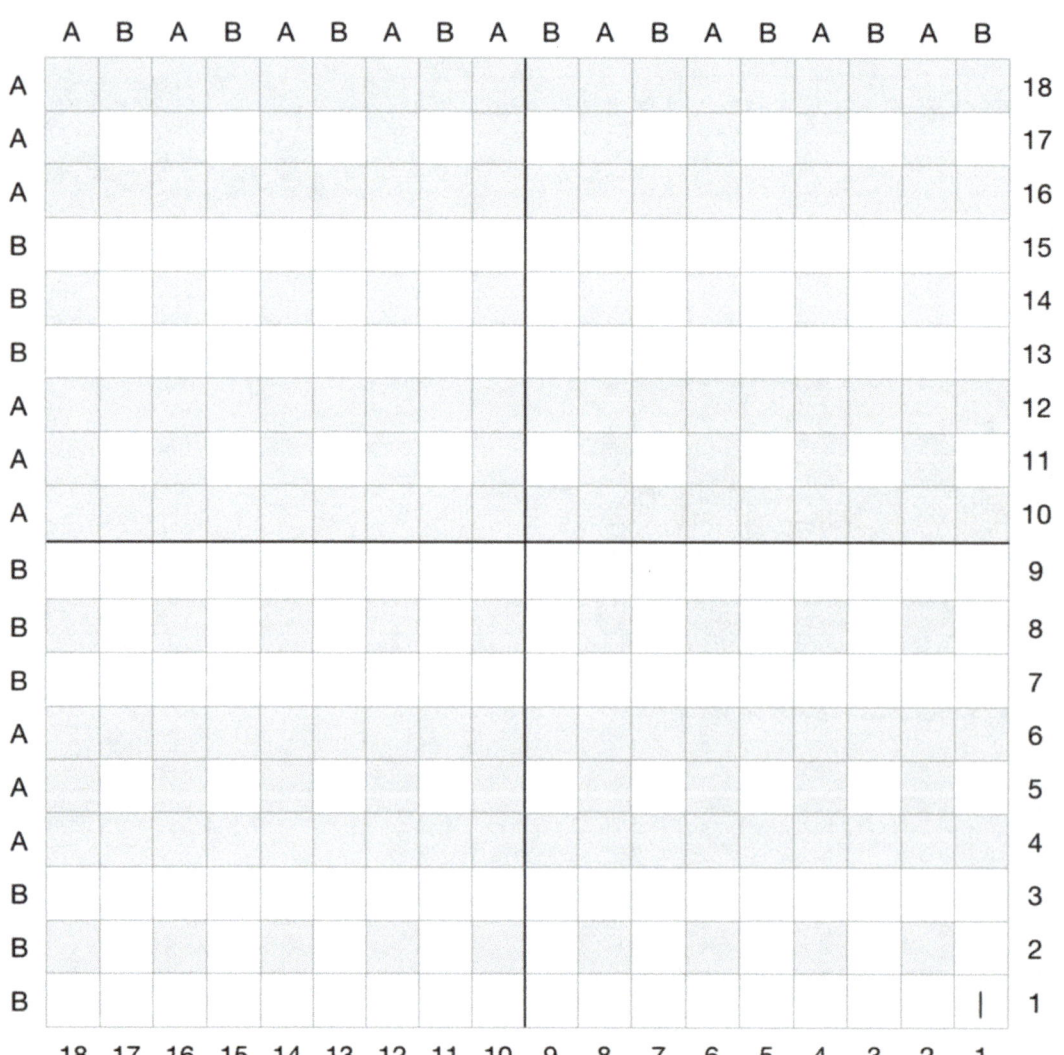

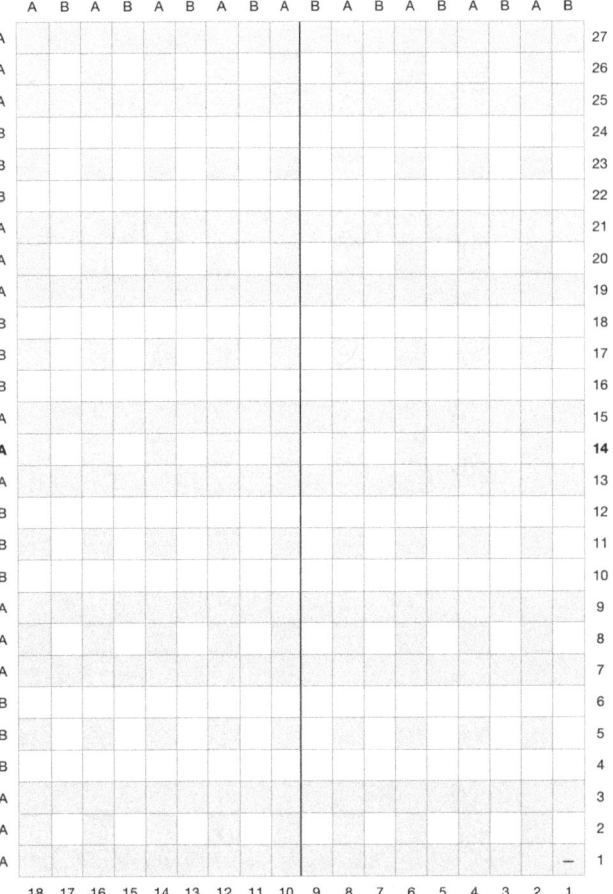

Pinwheel aka Puppy Tooth
Log Cabin AB/BA

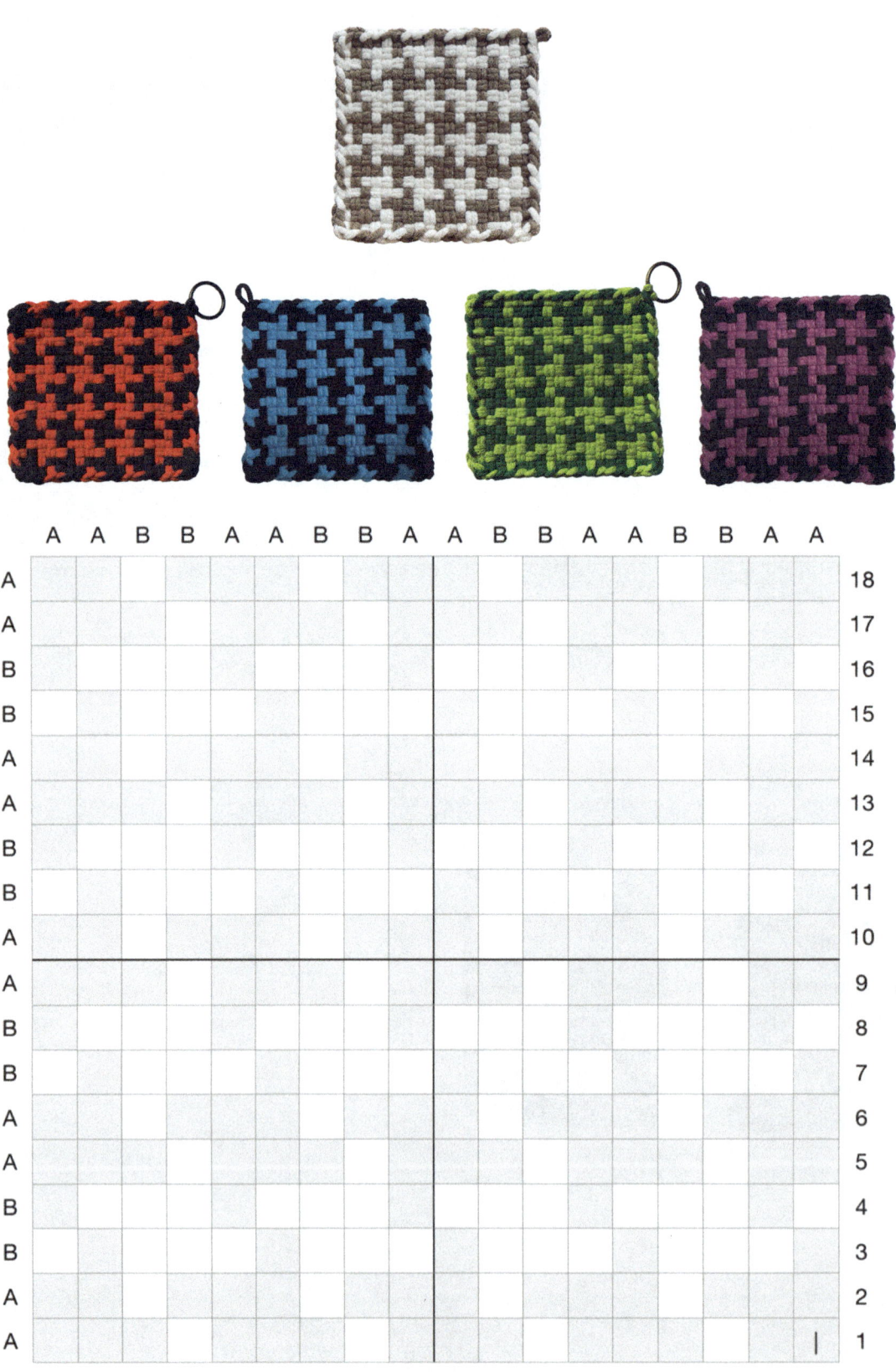

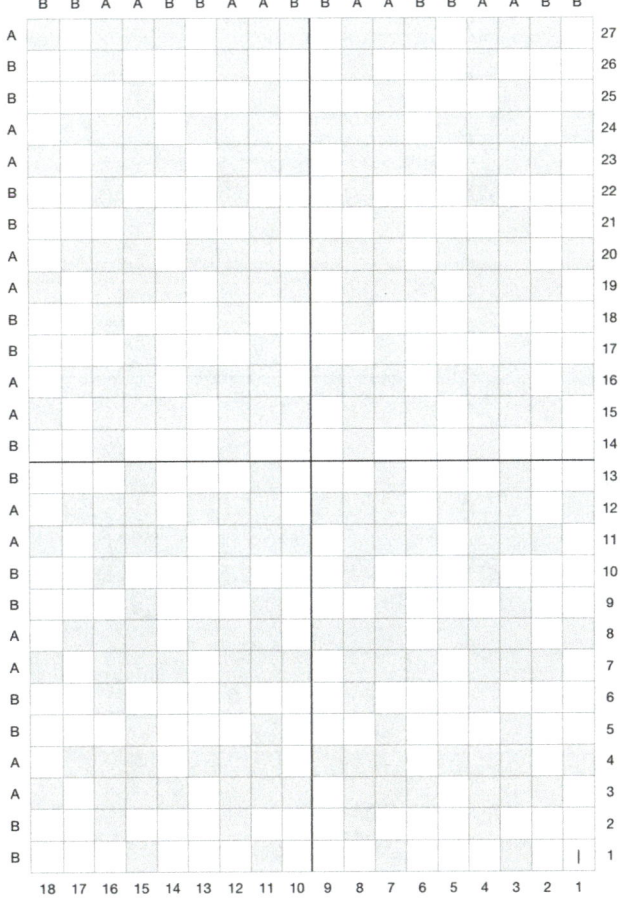

T

	B	A	B	B	A	B	B	A	B	B	A	B	B	A	B	B	A	B	
B																			18
A																			17
A																			16
B																			15
B																			14
A																			13
A																			12
B																			11
B																			10
A																			9
A																			8
B																			7
B																			6
A																			5
A																			4
B																			3
B																			2
A																			1
	18	17	16	15	14	13	12	11	10	9	8	7	6	5	4	3	2	1	

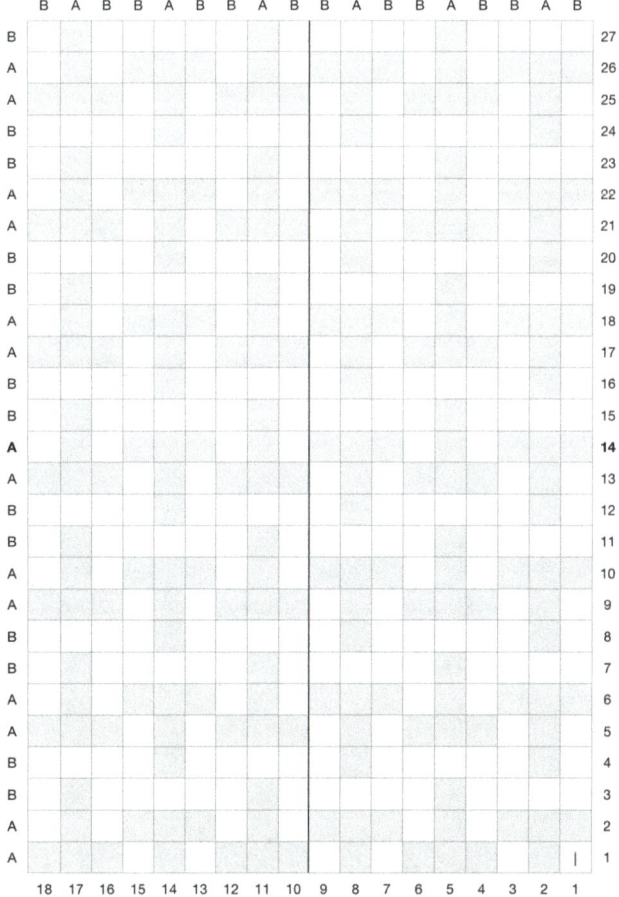

53

Zipper

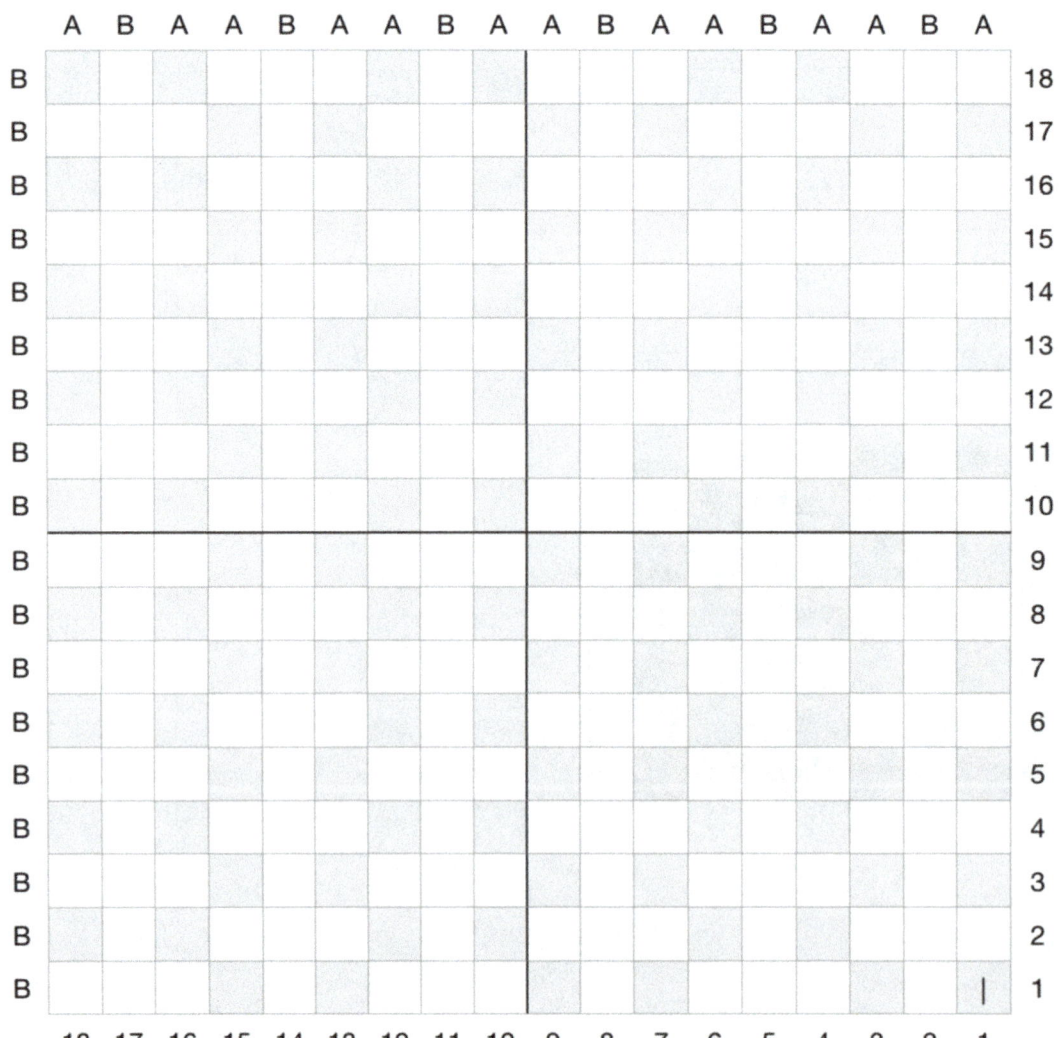

54

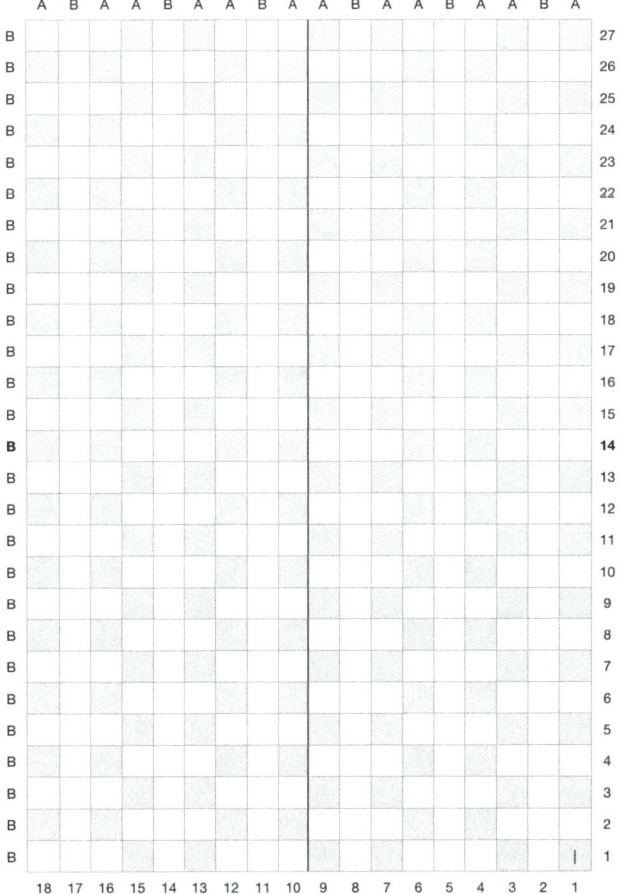

55

Equals
Log Cabin ABABA/ABABA

Human Rights Campaign Pansexual Transsexual Gay Marriage Equality

Bernie's Mitts
original design, Yavia Mirez

A = Autumn
W = Winter White
F = Flax
C = Chocolate

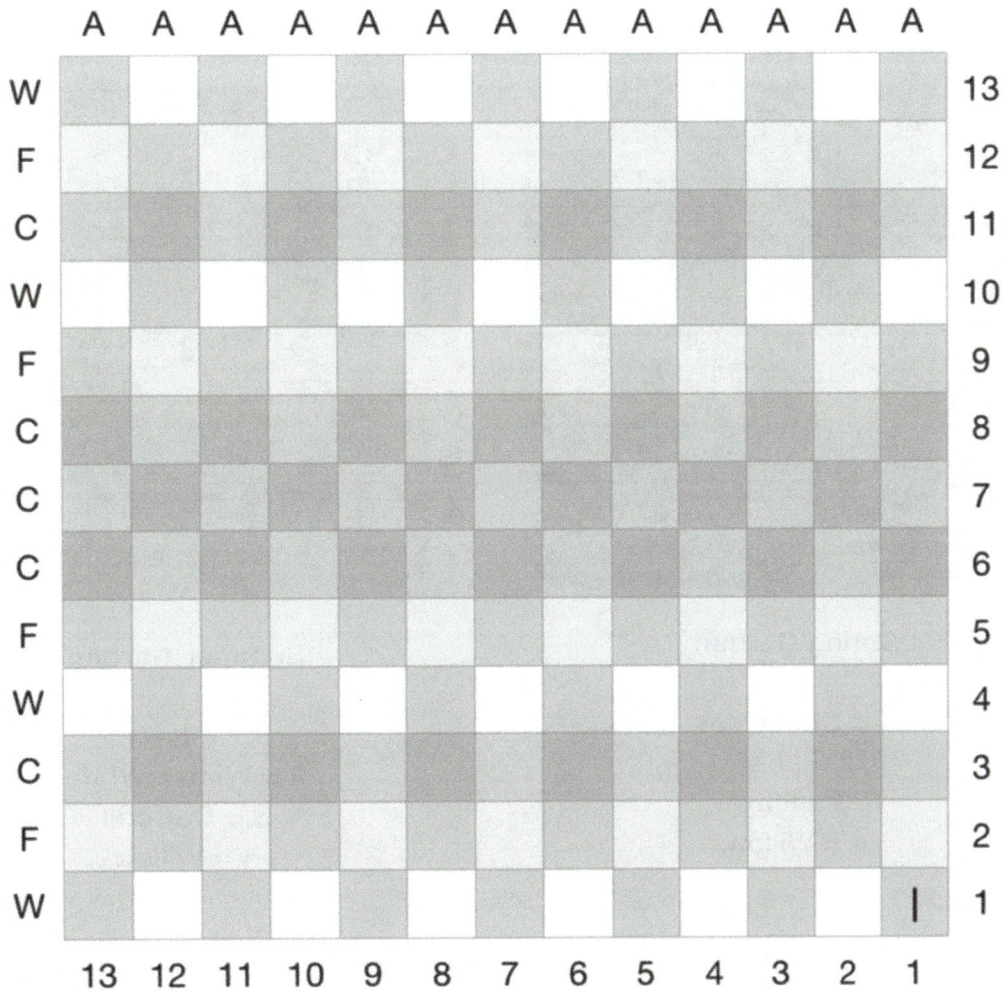

Christine's Garden Sampler
original design, Christine Olsen Reis

For the 27 peg loom, here are garden plans. Plain 18 peg potholders go well with this as a set. Try a winter and fall (harvest) garden as well!
Warp and weft are the same color sequence: warp then follow the warp sequence from the bottom up for your weft.

3	4	3	2	4	3	2	4	2	3	4	2	3	4	1	1	1	1	1	1	1	1	1	1	1	1	1

Spring Garden

1 = Chocolate
2 = Leaf
3 = Flax
4 = Willow

Summer Garden

1 = Leaf
2 = Winter White
3 = Daffodil
4 = Willow

CHAPTER 4

potholder patterns: shadow weave

Shadow weave is a subset of the general category color-and-weave, where the design is produced visually via the same alternating colors (or blocks of colors) in both warp and weft. Technically, shadow weave depends on two colors: log cabin is the simplest example of a shadow weave. The weaving structure is plain weave with a twill step at design changes. As you weave, you'll notice that rows will shadow each other in blocks of two: the second row will 'shadow' the first, reversing the direction of the pick. Not surprisingly, this produces a visual shadow effect in the fabric.

Shadow weave drafts seem to be well suited for conversion to potholder charts, yet there are very few potholder patterns available in shadow weave. To change the few to many, this chapter is the largest of the three pattern chapters. It's been a heady experience to find, choose, and chart shadow weave drafts; and the byproduct of this experience has been the emergence of original patterns. I hope that you'll find this a catalyst, as we have, opening an exciting creative door.

Box Chains
draft from handweaving.net, charted by Bill West

Corners
original design, Deborah Jean Cohen

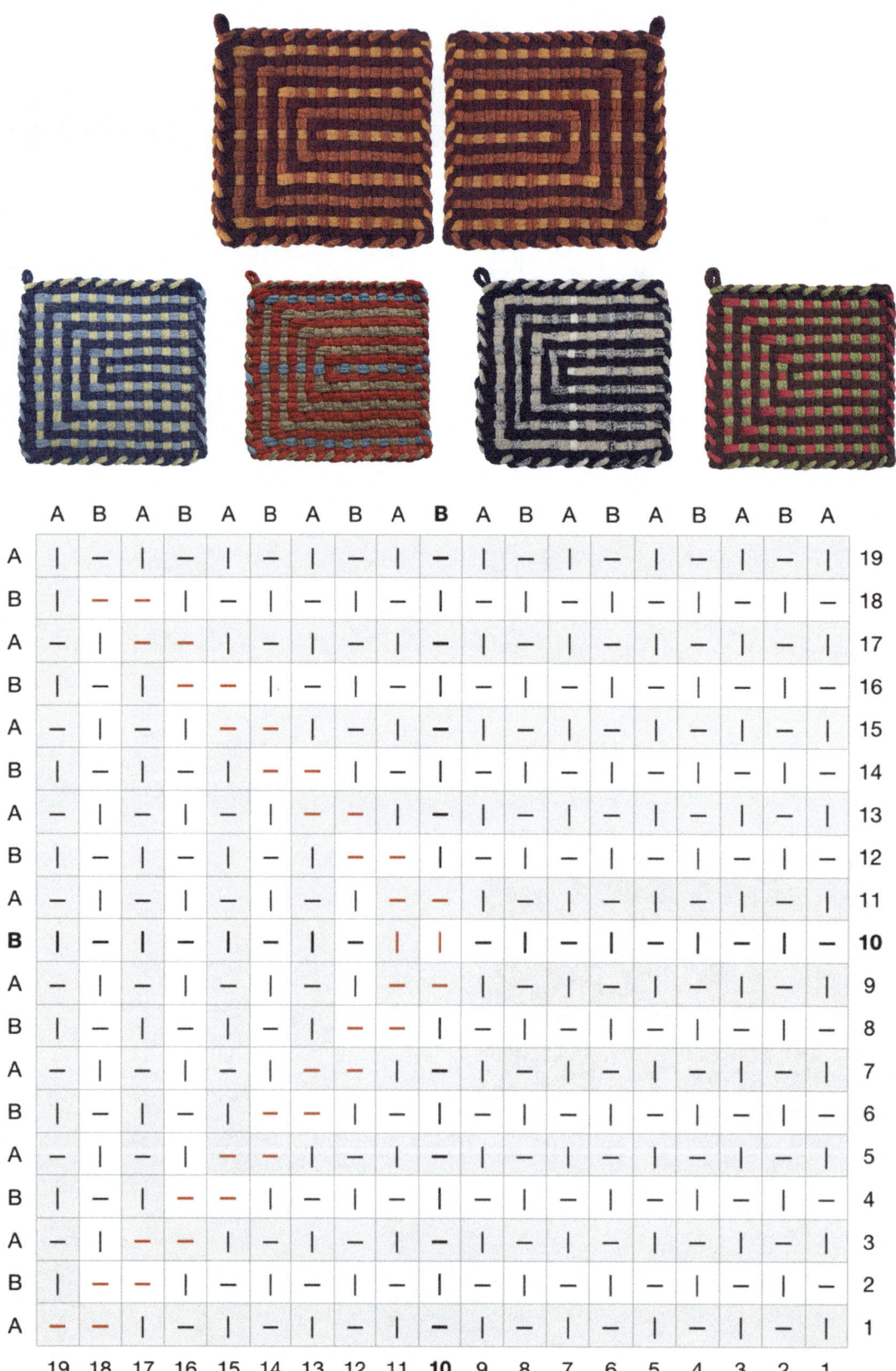

63

Apollo's Lyre
draft from handweaving.net, charted by Bill West

Circuitboard
draft from handweaving.net, charted by Bill West

Boxed Angles
draft from handweaving.net, charted by Bill West

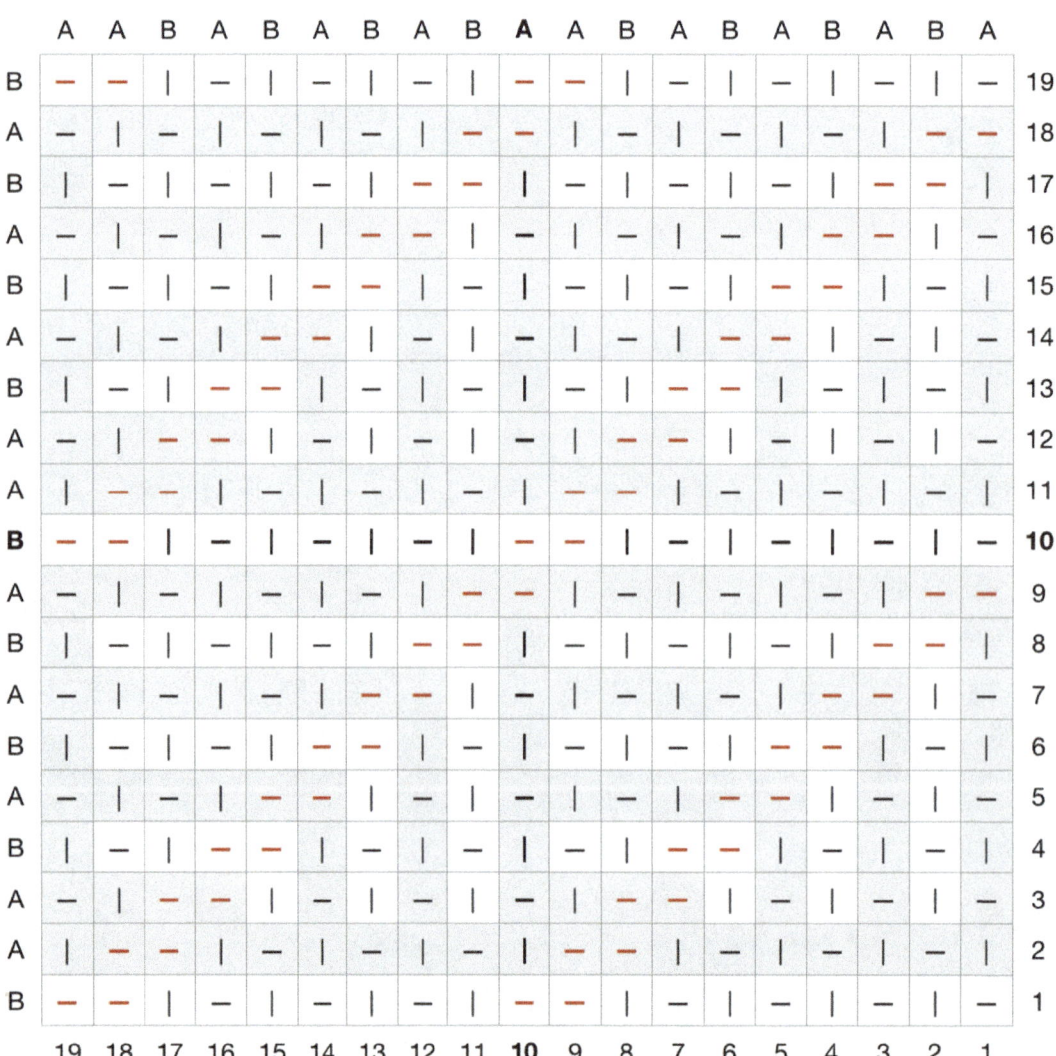

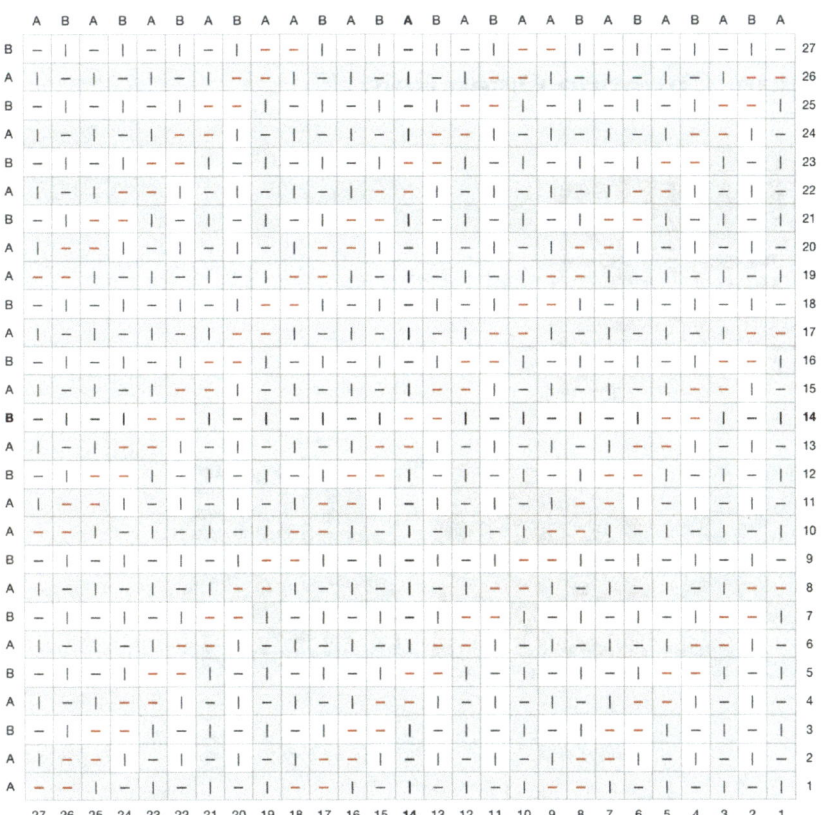

67

Escape

original design, Christine Olsen Reis

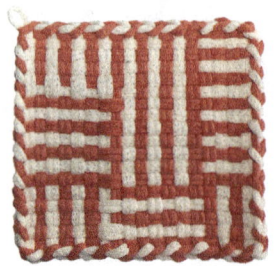

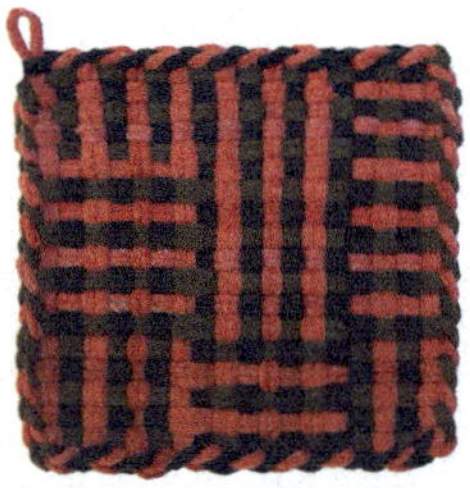
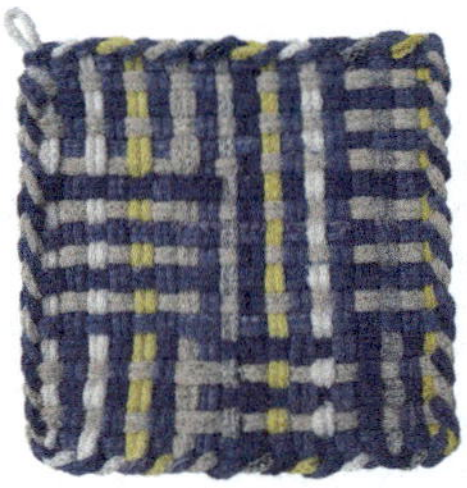
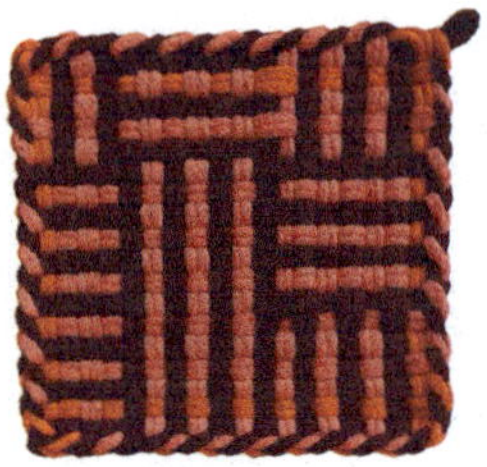
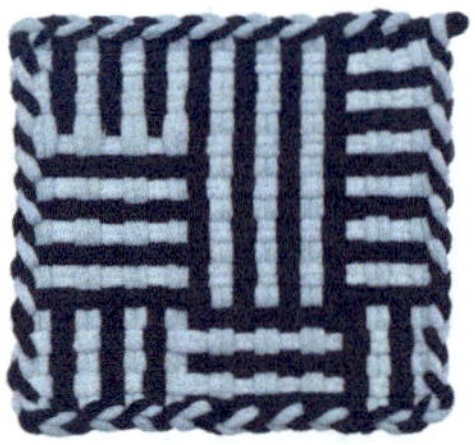

	B	A	B	A	B	A	B	A	B	A	B	A	B	A	A	B	A	B	
A	|	—	|	—	|	—	|	—	|	—	|	—	|	—	|	—	|	—	18
B	—	|	—	|	—	|	—	|	—	|	—	|	—	|	—	|	—	|	17
A	|	—	|	—	|	—	|	—	|	—	|	—	|	—	|	—	|	—	16
B	—	|	—	|	—	|	—	|	—	|	—	|	—	|	—	|	—	|	15
A	|	—	|	—	|	—	|	—	|	—	|	—	|	—	|	—	|	—	14
B	|	—	|	—	|	—	|	|	—	|	—	|	—	|	—	|	—	|	13
A	—	|	—	|	—	|	—	—	|	—	|	—	|	—	|	—	|	—	12
B	|	—	|	—	|	—	|	|	—	|	—	|	—	|	—	|	—	|	11
A	—	|	—	|	—	|	—	—	|	—	|	—	|	—	|	—	|	—	10
B	|	—	|	—	|	—	|	|	—	|	—	|	—	|	—	|	—	|	9
A	—	|	—	|	—	|	—	—	|	—	|	—	|	—	|	—	|	—	8
B	|	—	|	—	|	—	|	|	—	|	—	|	—	|	—	|	—	|	7
A	—	|	—	|	—	|	—	—	|	—	|	—	|	—	|	—	|	—	6
A	|	—	|	—	|	—	|	|	—	|	—	|	—	|	—	|	—	|	5
B	—	|	—	|	—	|	—	—	|	—	|	—	|	—	|	—	|	—	4
A	|	—	|	—	|	—	|	|	—	|	—	|	—	|	—	|	—	|	3
B	—	|	—	|	—	|	—	—	|	—	|	—	|	—	|	—	|	—	2
A	|	—	|	—	|	—	|	|	—	|	—	|	—	|	—	|	—	|	1
	18	17	16	15	14	13	12	11	10	9	8	7	6	5	4	3	2	1	

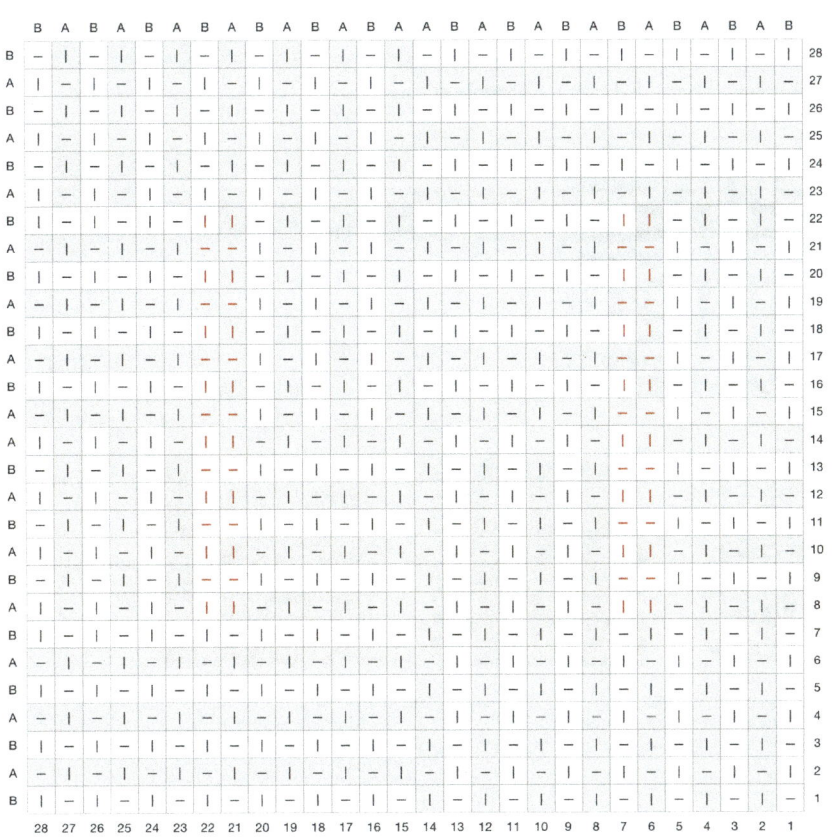

69

Facets
original design, Mary Clarke

	A	B	A	B	A	B	A	B	A	A	B	A	B	A	B	A	B	A	B	
A	—	—	|	—	|	—	|	—	|	—	|	—	|	—	|	—	|	—	|	19
B	|	—	—	|	—	|	—	|	—	|	—	|	—	|	—	|	—	|	—	18
A	—	|	—	—	|	—	|	—	|	—	|	—	|	—	|	—	|	—	|	17
B	|	—	|	—	—	|	—	|	—	|	—	|	—	|	—	|	—	|	—	16
A	—	|	—	|	—	—	|	—	|	—	|	—	|	—	|	—	|	—	|	15
B	|	—	|	—	|	—	—	|	—	|	—	|	—	|	—	|	—	|	—	14
A	—	|	—	|	—	|	—	—	|	—	|	—	|	—	|	—	|	—	|	13
B	|	—	|	—	|	—	|	—	—	|	—	|	—	|	—	|	—	|	—	12
A	—	|	—	|	—	|	—	|	—	—	|	—	|	—	|	—	|	—	|	11
A	|	—	|	—	|	—	|	—	|	—	—	|	—	|	—	|	—	|	—	10
B	|	—	|	—	|	—	|	—	|	—	—	|	—	|	—	|	—	|	9
A	—	|	—	|	—	|	—	|	—	|	—	—	|	—	|	—	|	—	8
B	|	—	|	—	|	—	|	—	|	—	|	—	—	|	—	|	—	|	7
A	—	|	—	|	—	|	—	|	—	|	—	|	—	—	|	—	|	—	6
B	—	—	|	—	|	—	|	—	|	—	|	—	|	—	—	|	—	|	5
A	|	—	|	—	|	—	|	—	|	—	|	—	|	—	—	|	—	|	4
B	—	|	—	|	—	|	—	|	—	|	—	|	—	|	—	—	|	—	3
A	|	—	|	—	|	—	|	—	|	—	|	—	|	—	|	—	—	|	2
B	—	|	—	|	—	|	—	|	—	|	—	|	—	|	—	|	—	—	1
	19	18	17	16	15	14	13	12	11	10	9	8	7	6	5	4	3	2	1	

71

Fillet
original design, Mary Clarke

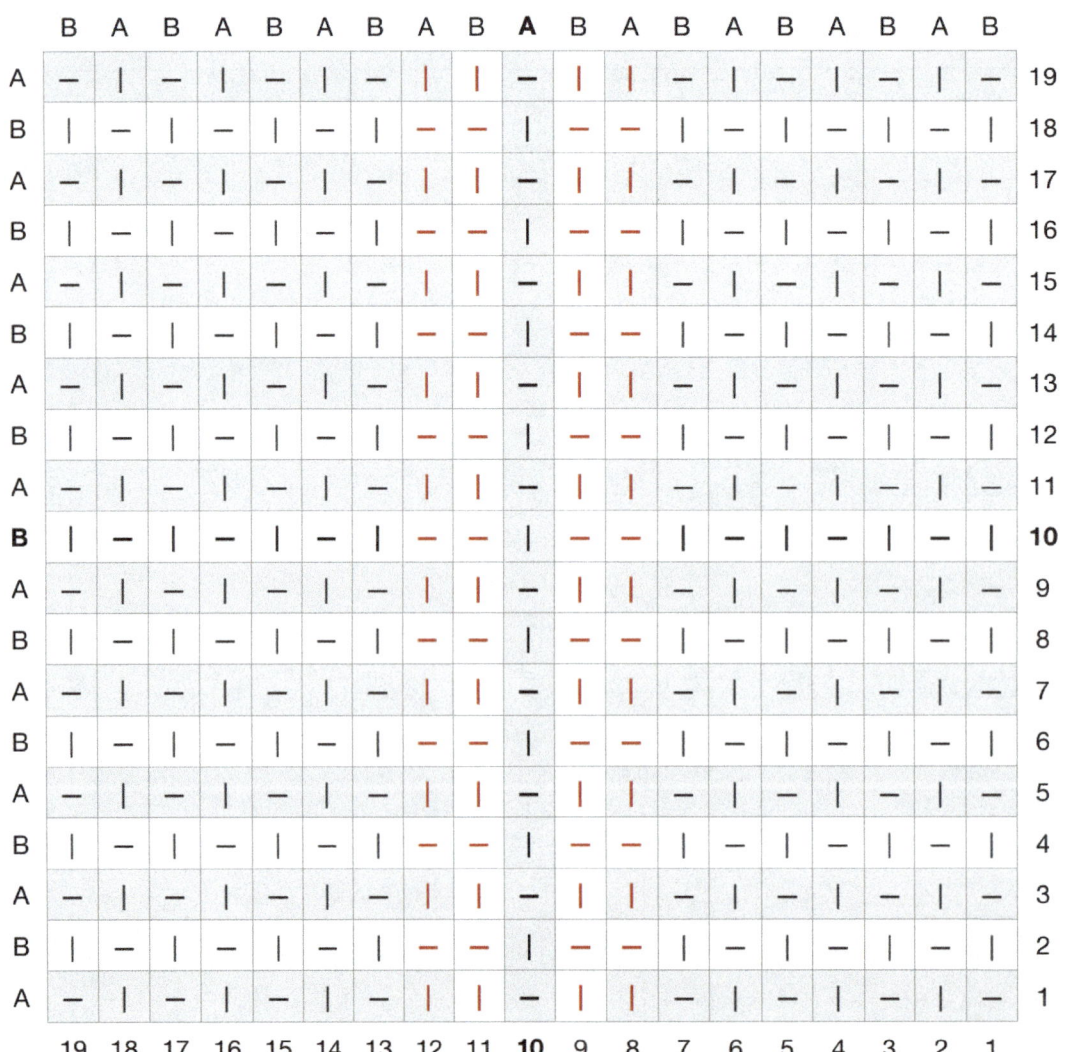

Mixing loops adds texture and variety, plus is interesting and a lot of fun. The first potholder in the row on the facing page is woven from Harrisville Designs Spice and Pepperell variegated dark colors. The second uses Harrisville Designs Turquoise and Green, with the green from different dye lots. The third is dyed Harrisville Designs White (with RIT Daffodil) and Green, also from different dye lots. And the last of the row is Harrisville Designs Blue and loops cut from socks that my husband didn't like and never wore.

Below left is Harrisville Designs Pink, Autumn, and Burgundy. Below right is Harrisville Designs Red and Wool Novelty Company white.

Four Corners
a mashup of Right Angles and Boxed Angles, Deborah Jean Cohen

Shadow Diamond
draft from handweaving.com, charted by Deborah Jean Cohen

Greek Courtyard
draft from handweaving.com, charted by Deborah Jean Cohen

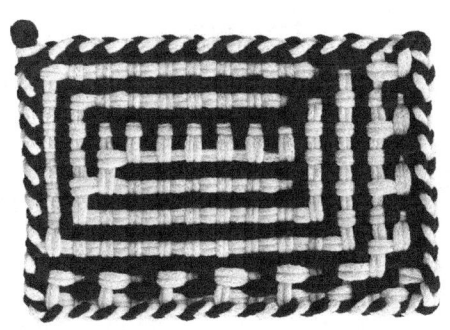

Infinite
original design, Christine Olsen Reis

Looking Through Barred Windows
draft from handweaving.net, charted by Bill West

Shadow Cross
draft from handweaving.com, charted by Christine Olsen Reis

On the loom.

Off the loom.

Front.

Back.

Loop de Loop
original design, Christine Olsen Reis

	A	A	B	A	B	A	B	A	B	**A**	A	B	A	B	A	B	A	B	A	
A	—	|	—	|	—	|	—	|	—	|	—	|	—	|	—	|	—	|	—	19
B	—	—	|	—	|	—	|	—	|	—	|	—	|	—	|	—	|	—	|	18
A	|	—	—	|	—	|	—	|	—	|	—	|	—	|	—	|	—	|	—	17
B	—	|	—	—	|	—	|	—	|	—	|	—	|	—	|	—	|	—	|	16
A	|	—	|	—	—	|	—	|	—	|	—	|	—	|	—	|	—	|	—	15
B	—	|	—	|	—	—	|	—	|	—	|	—	|	—	|	—	|	—	|	14
A	|	—	|	—	|	—	—	|	—	|	—	|	—	|	—	|	—	|	—	13
B	—	|	—	|	—	|	—	—	|	—	|	—	|	—	|	—	|	—	|	12
A	|	—	|	—	|	—	|	—	—	|	—	|	—	|	—	|	—	|	—	11
A	—	|	—	|	—	|	—	|	—	—	|	—	|	—	|	—	|	—	|	**10**
B	|	—	|	—	|	—	|	—	|	—	—	|	—	|	—	|	—	|	—	9
A	—	|	—	|	—	|	—	|	—	|	—	—	|	—	|	—	|	—	|	8
B	|	—	|	—	|	—	|	—	|	—	|	—	—	|	—	|	—	|	—	7
A	—	|	—	|	—	|	—	|	—	|	—	|	—	—	|	—	|	—	|	6
B	|	—	|	—	|	—	|	—	|	—	|	—	|	—	—	|	—	|	—	5
A	—	|	—	|	—	|	—	|	—	|	—	|	—	|	—	—	|	—	|	4
B	|	—	|	—	|	—	|	—	|	—	|	—	|	—	|	—	—	|	—	3
A	—	|	—	|	—	|	—	|	—	|	—	|	—	|	—	|	—	—	|	2
A	|	—	|	—	|	—	|	—	|	—	|	—	|	—	|	—	|	—	—	1
	19	18	17	16	15	14	13	12	11	**10**	9	8	7	6	5	4	3	2	1	

Maze in a Diamond
draft from handweaving.com, charted by Bill West

Maze of Enigma
original design, Bill West

Multicursal Maze
original design, Bill West

	B	A	B	A	B	A	B	A	B	A	B	A	B	A	B	A	B	A	
B	–	|	–	|	–	|	–	|	|	–	|	–	|	–	|	–	|	18
A	|	–	|	–	|	–	|	–	–	|	|	–	|	–	|	–	|	17
B	–	|	–	|	–	|	–	|	–	–	|	–	|	–	|	–	|	16
A	|	–	|	–	|	–	|	–	|	|	–	–	|	–	|	–	–	15
B	|	|	–	|	–	|	–	|	–	–	|	–	|	–	|	|	|	14
A	–	–	|	–	|	–	|	–	|	|	–	|	–	|	–	–	–	13
B	–	|	–	|	–	|	–	|	|	–	|	–	|	–	–	–	|	12
A	|	–	|	–	|	–	|	–	|	–	–	|	–	–	|	–	|	11
B	–	|	–	|	|	–	|	–	|	|	–	|	–	|	–	|	–	10
A	|	–	|	|	–	–	|	–	|	–	|	–	|	–	|	|	–	9
B	–	|	–	|	|	–	|	–	|	–	|	–	|	–	|	|	–	8
A	|	|	–	|	–	|	–	|	–	|	–	|	–	|	–	|	|	7
B	–	–	|	–	|	–	|	|	–	|	–	|	–	|	–	–	–	6
A	|	–	|	–	|	–	|	–	|	–	|	–	|	–	|	–	|	5
B	–	|	|	–	|	–	–	|	–	|	–	|	–	|	–	|	–	4
A	|	–	|	|	–	–	|	–	|	–	|	–	|	–	|	–	|	3
B	–	|	–	|	–	|	–	|	|	–	|	–	|	–	|	–	|	2
A	|	–	|	–	|	–	|	–	|	–	–	|	–	|	–	|	–	1
	18	17	16	15	14	13	12	11	10	9	8	7	6	5	4	3	2	1	

Opening
original design, Christine Olsen Reis

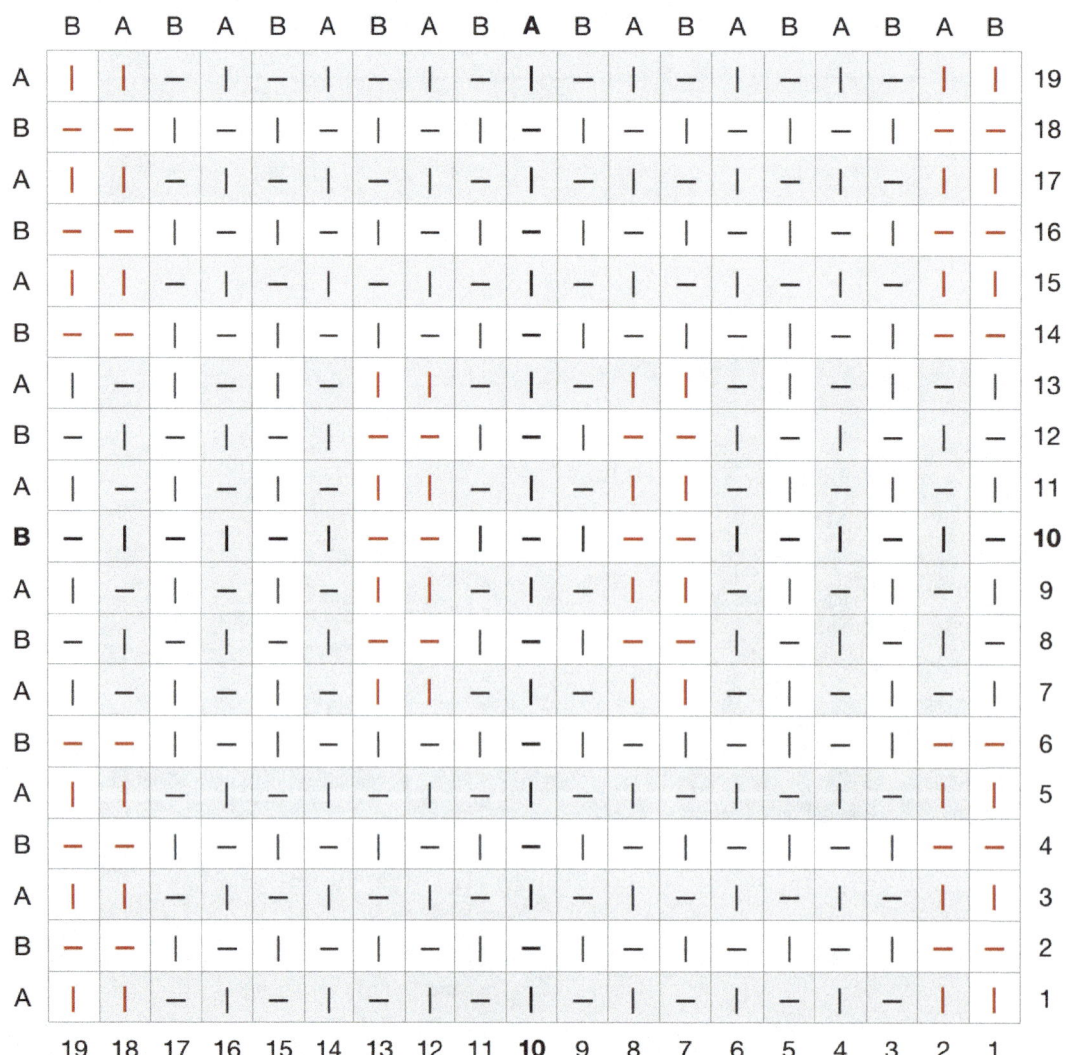

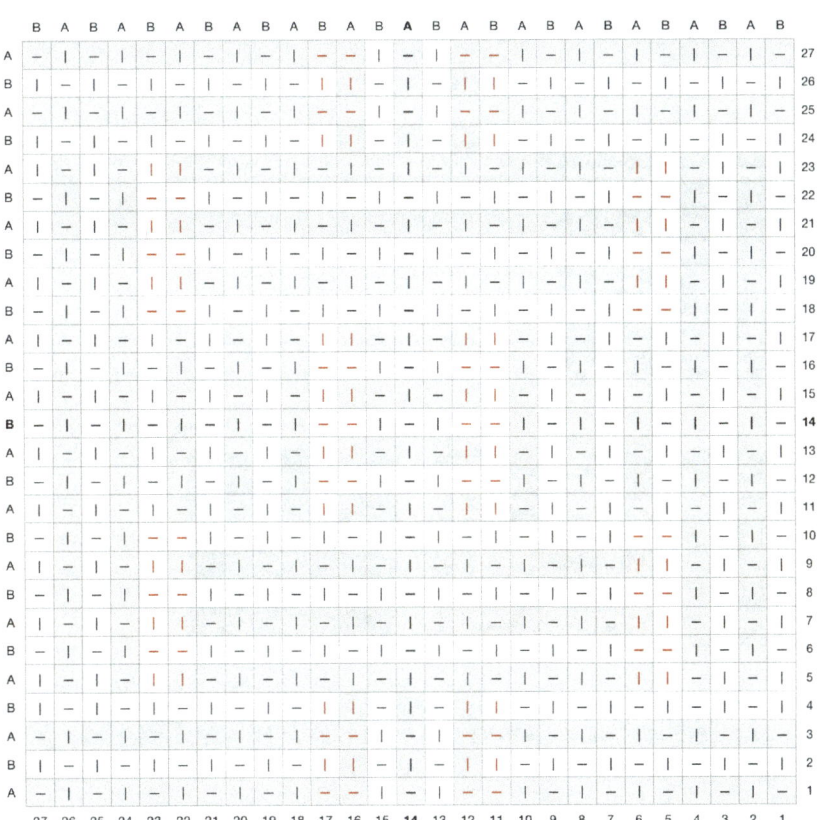

Ramble
original design, Mary Clarke

	B	A	B	A	B	A	B	A	B	A	B	A	B	A	B	A	B	A	
A	|	–	–	|	–	|	–	|	–	|	–	|	–	|	–	|	–	–	18
B	–	|	–	–	|	–	|	–	|	–	|	–	|	–	|	–	–	|	17
A	|	–	|	–	|	–	|	–	|	–	|	–	|	–	|	–	–	|	–	16
B	–	|	–	|	–	|	–	|	–	|	–	|	–	|	–	–	|	–	|	15
A	|	–	|	–	–	|	–	|	–	|	–	–	|	–	|	–	|	–	14
B	–	|	–	|	–	|	|	–	|	–	–	|	–	|	–	|	–	|	13
A	|	–	|	–	|	|	–	|	–	|	–	–	|	–	|	–	|	–	12
B	–	|	–	|	–	–	|	–	|	–	|	–	|	–	|	–	|	11
A	|	–	|	–	–	|	–	|	|	–	|	–	|	–	|	–	|	–	10
B	–	–	|	–	|	–	|	–	–	|	–	|	–	|	–	|	–	|	9
A	|	|	–	|	–	|	–	|	–	–	|	–	|	–	|	–	|	–	8
B	–	–	|	–	|	–	|	|	–	|	–	|	–	|	–	|	–	|	7
A	|	–	|	–	|	–	–	|	–	|	–	|	–	|	–	|	–	6
B	–	|	–	|	|	–	|	–	|	–	|	–	|	–	|	–	|	5
A	|	–	|	|	–	|	–	|	–	|	–	|	–	|	–	–	|	4
B	–	|	–	|	–	|	–	|	–	|	–	|	–	|	–	–	|	3
A	|	–	–	|	–	|	–	|	–	|	–	|	–	|	–	–	|	2
B	–	–	|	–	|	–	|	–	|	–	|	–	|	–	–	–	|	1
	18	17	16	15	14	13	12	11	10	9	8	7	6	5	4	3	2	1	

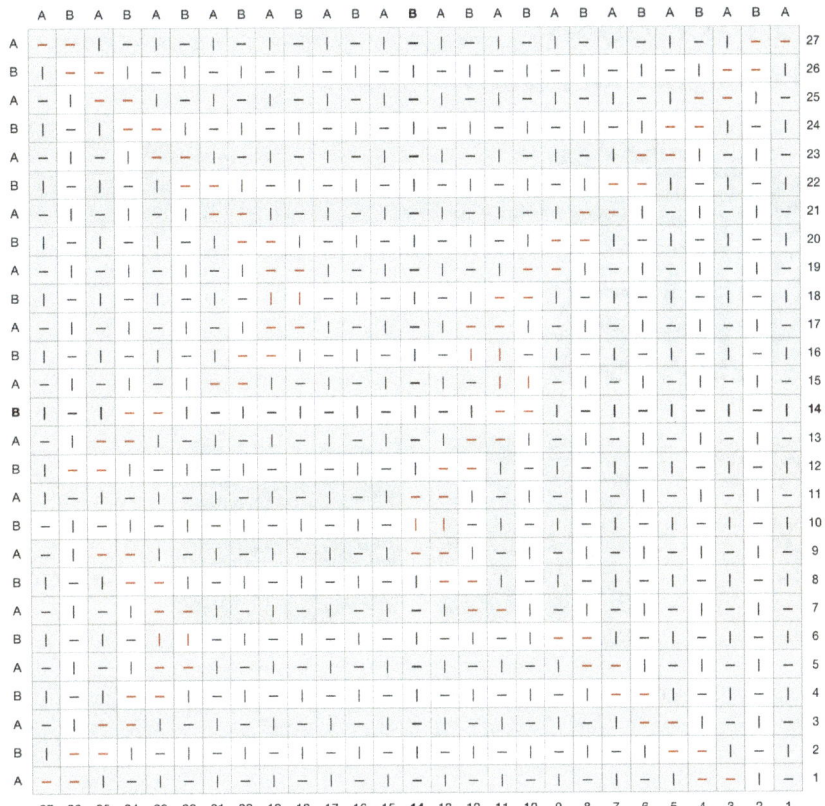

The original Green-and-black Weirdo

Right Angles
original design, Mary Clarke

	B	A	B	A	B	A	B	A	B	A	B	A	B	A	B	A	B	A	
B	—	—	|	—	|	—	|	—	|	—	|	—	|	—	|	—	|	—	18
A	|	—	—	|	—	|	—	|	—	|	—	|	—	|	—	|	—	|	17
B	—	|	—	—	|	—	|	—	|	—	|	—	|	—	|	—	|	—	16
A	|	—	|	—	—	|	—	|	—	|	—	|	—	|	—	|	—	|	15
B	—	|	—	|	—	—	|	—	|	—	|	—	|	—	|	—	|	—	14
A	|	—	|	—	|	—	—	|	—	|	—	|	—	|	—	|	—	|	13
B	—	|	—	|	—	|	—	—	|	—	|	—	|	—	|	—	|	—	12
A	|	—	|	—	|	—	|	—	—	|	—	|	—	|	—	|	—	|	11
B	—	|	—	|	—	|	—	|	—	—	|	—	|	—	|	—	|	—	10
A	|	—	|	—	|	—	|	—	|	—	—	|	—	|	—	|	—	|	9
B	—	|	—	|	—	|	—	|	—	|	—	—	|	—	|	—	|	—	8
A	|	—	|	—	|	—	|	—	|	—	|	—	—	|	—	|	—	|	7
B	—	|	—	|	—	|	—	|	—	|	—	|	—	—	|	—	|	—	6
A	|	—	|	—	|	—	|	—	|	—	|	—	|	—	—	|	—	|	5
B	—	|	—	|	—	|	—	|	—	|	—	|	—	|	—	—	|	—	4
A	|	—	|	—	|	—	|	—	|	—	|	—	|	—	|	—	—	|	3
B	—	|	—	|	—	|	—	|	—	|	—	|	—	|	—	|	—	—	2
A	|	—	|	—	|	—	|	—	|	—	|	—	|	—	|	—	|	—	1
	18	17	16	15	14	13	12	11	10	9	8	7	6	5	4	3	2	1	

93

Right-angle Hitch
original design, Mary Clarke

	A	B	A	B	A	B	A	B	A	A	B	A	B	A	B	A	B	A	
B	−	|	−	|	−	|	−	|	−	|	−	|	−	|	−	|	−	|	18
A	−	−	|	−	|	−	|	−	|	−	|	−	|	−	|	−	|	−	17
B	|	−	−	|	−	|	−	|	−	|	−	|	−	|	−	|	−	|	16
A	−	|	−	−	|	−	|	−	|	−	|	−	|	−	|	−	|	−	15
B	|	−	|	−	−	|	−	|	−	|	−	|	−	|	−	|	−	|	14
A	−	|	−	|	−	−	|	−	|	−	|	−	|	−	|	−	|	−	13
B	|	−	|	−	|	−	−	|	−	|	−	|	−	|	−	|	−	|	12
A	−	|	−	|	−	|	−	−	|	−	|	−	|	−	|	−	|	−	11
B	|	−	|	−	|	−	|	−	−	|	−	|	−	|	−	|	−	|	10
A	−	|	−	|	−	|	−	|	−	−	|	−	|	−	|	−	|	−	9
B	|	−	|	−	|	−	|	−	|	−	−	|	−	|	−	|	−	|	8
A	−	|	−	|	−	|	−	|	−	|	−	−	|	−	|	−	|	−	7
B	|	−	|	−	|	−	|	−	|	−	|	−	−	|	−	|	−	|	6
A	−	|	−	|	−	|	−	|	−	|	−	|	−	−	|	−	|	−	5
B	|	−	|	−	|	−	|	−	|	−	|	−	|	−	−	|	−	|	4
A	−	|	−	|	−	|	−	|	−	|	−	|	−	|	−	−	|	−	3
B	|	−	|	−	|	−	|	−	|	−	|	−	|	−	|	−	−	|	2
A	−	|	−	|	−	|	−	|	−	|	−	|	−	|	−	|	−	−	1
	18	17	16	15	14	13	12	11	10	9	8	7	6	5	4	3	2	1	

Shadow Aztec
draft from handweaving.net, charted by Deborah Jean Cohen

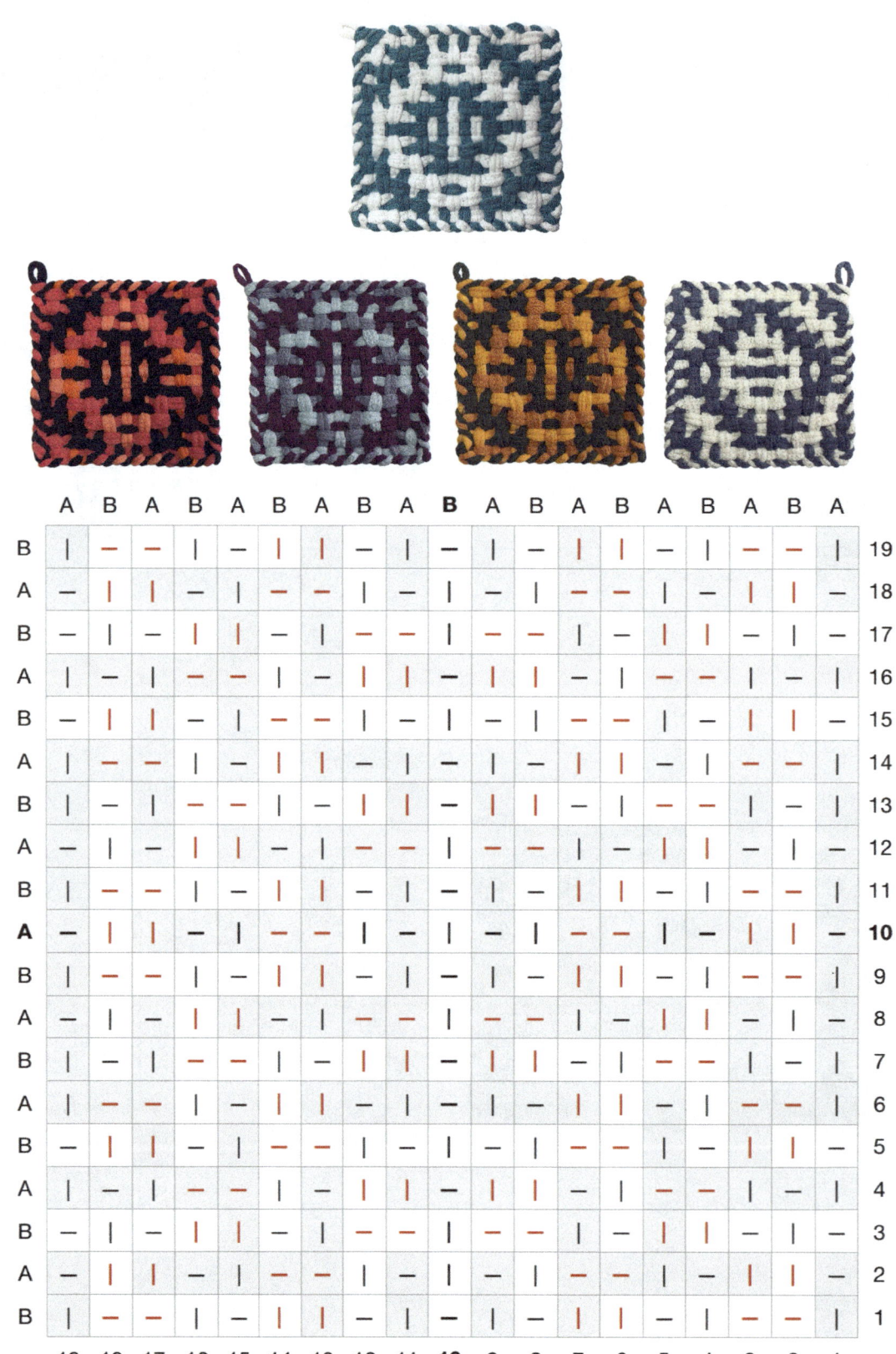

Woven with the weft colors reversed.

Woven with weft colors reversed, and multiple colors for B.

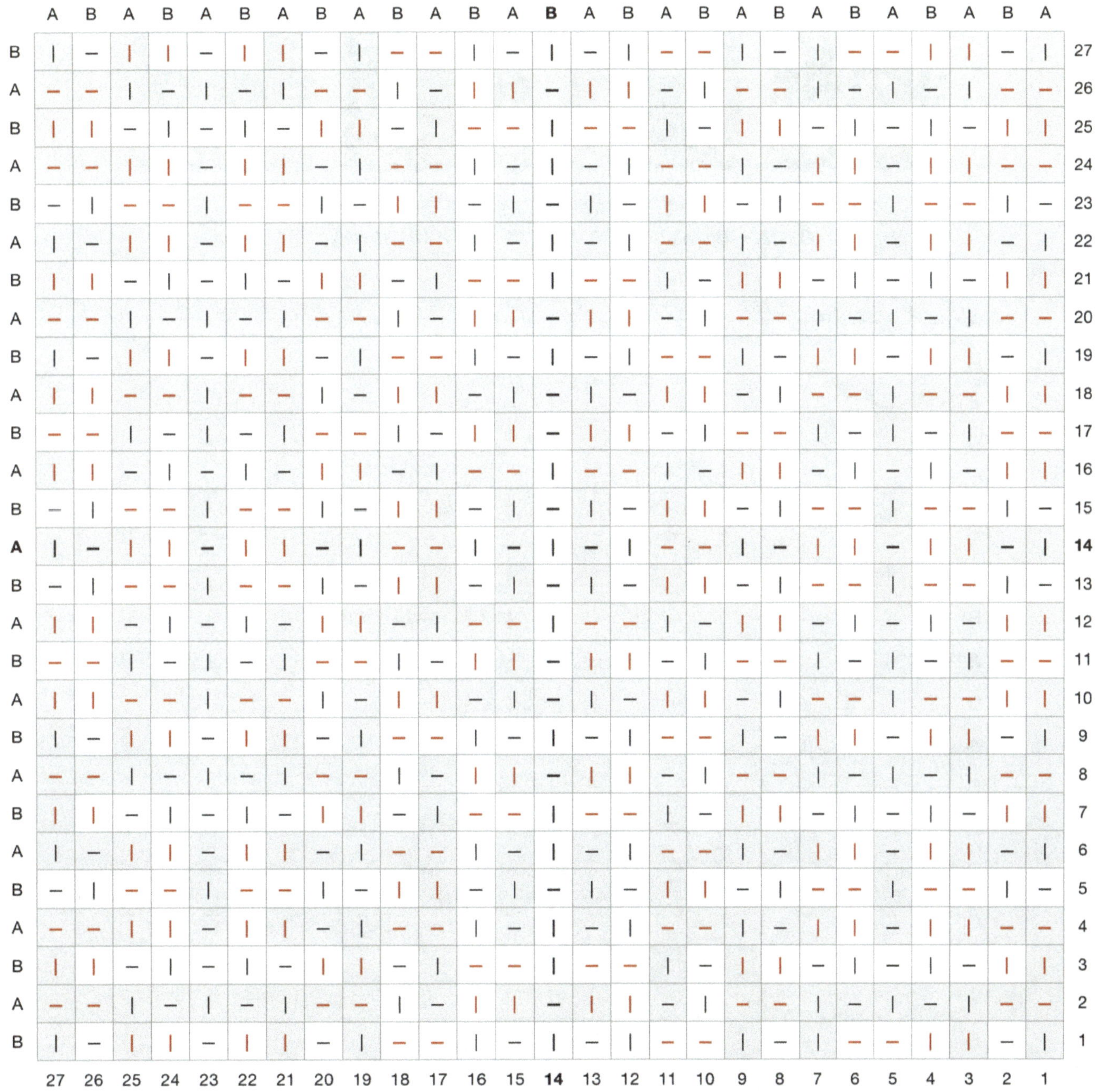

97

Shadow Baseball Diamond
draft from handweaving.net, charted by Bill West

Shadow Aztec (above left) and Shadow Baseball Diamond (above right) are similar enough to make a nice set.

Shadow Fern
draft from handweaving.net, charted by Deborah Jean Cohen

Shadow Kelp
draft from handweaving.net, charted by Deborah Jean Cohen

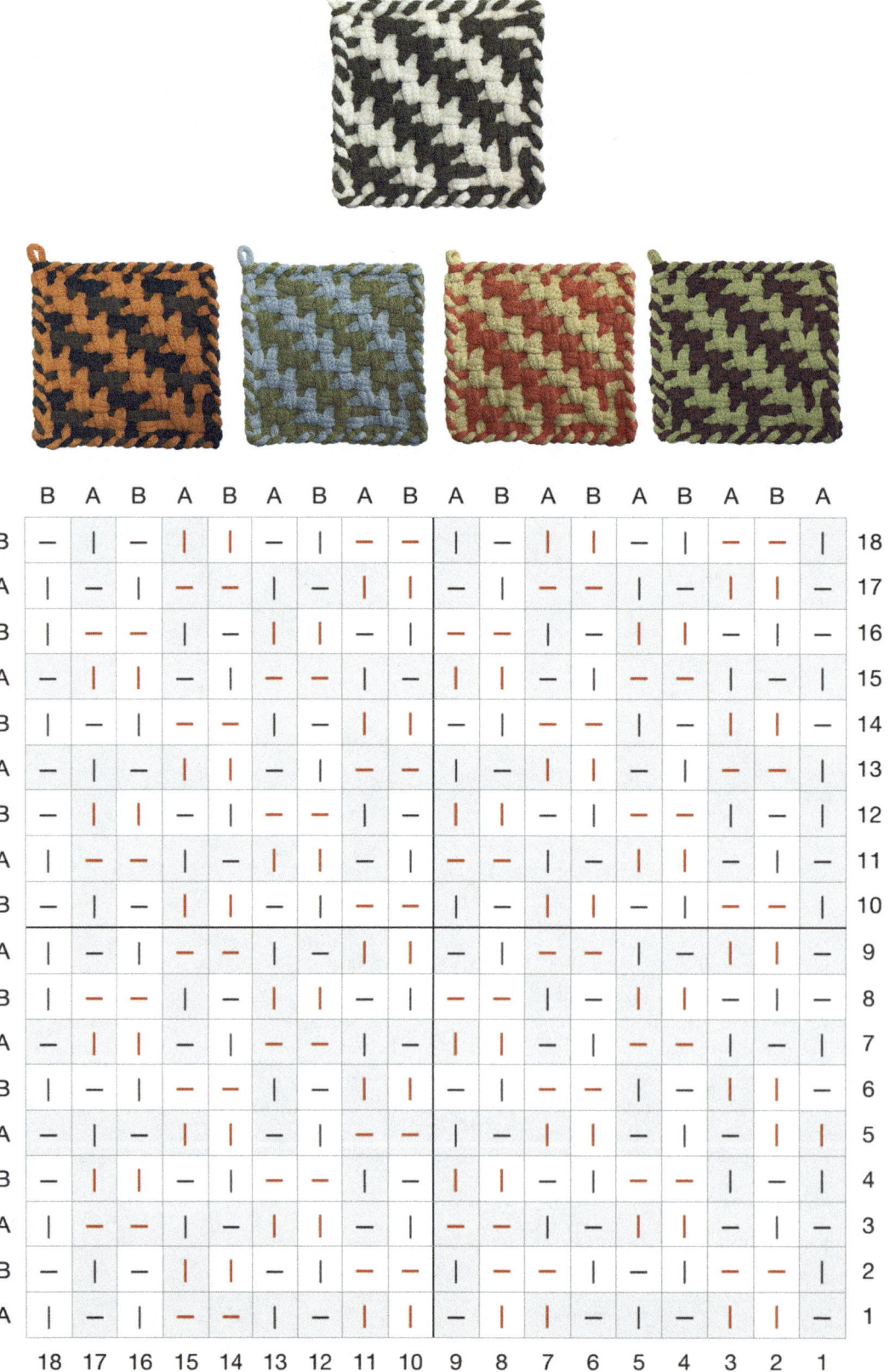

Whirling Logs
original design, Deborah Jean Cohen

Shadow Seaweed 2
draft from handweaving.net, charted by Deborah Jean Cohen

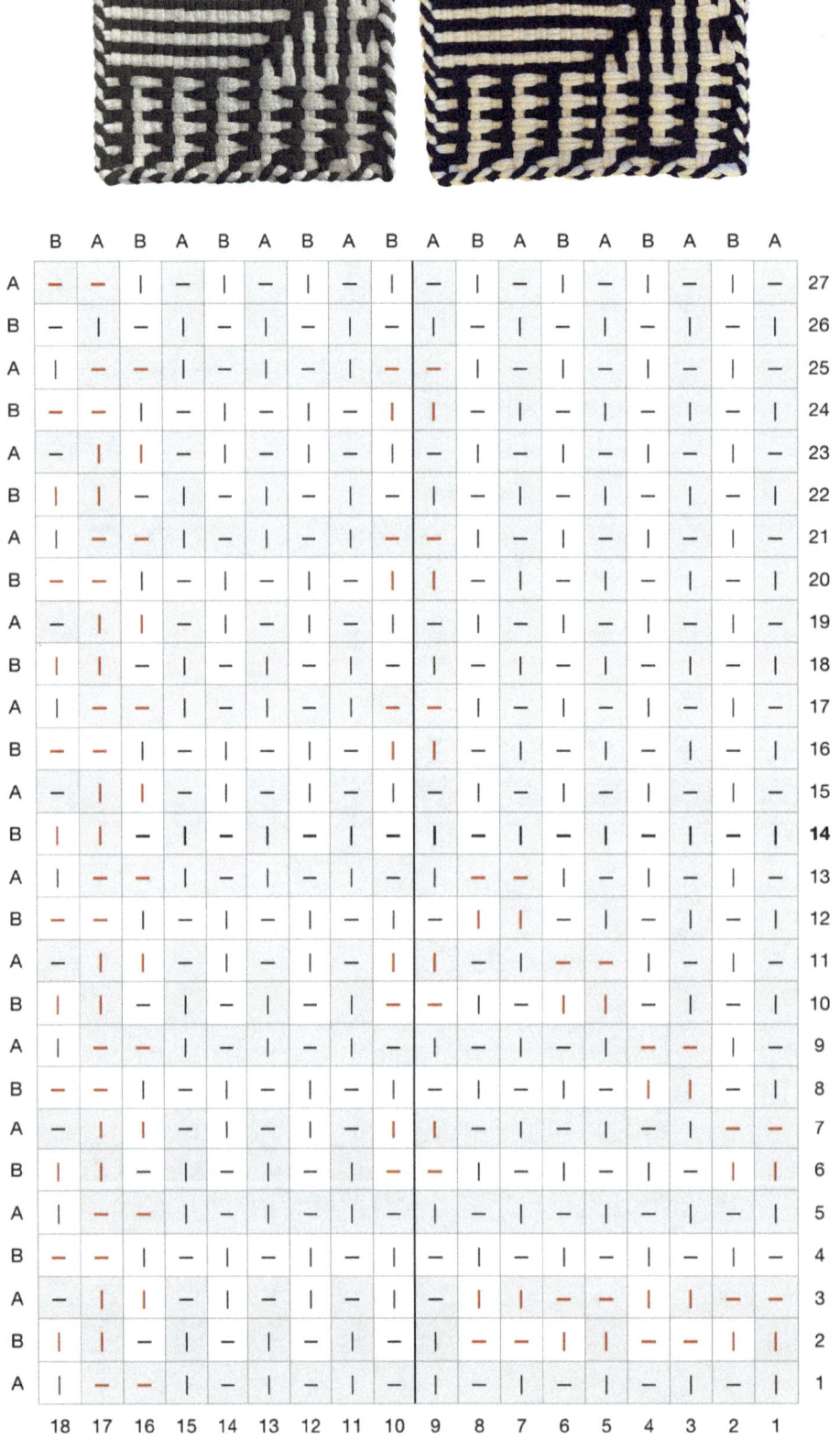

Shadow Seaweed 3
draft from handweaving.net, charted by Deborah Jean Cohen

Shadow Seaweed
draft from handweaving.net, charted by Deborah Jean Cohen

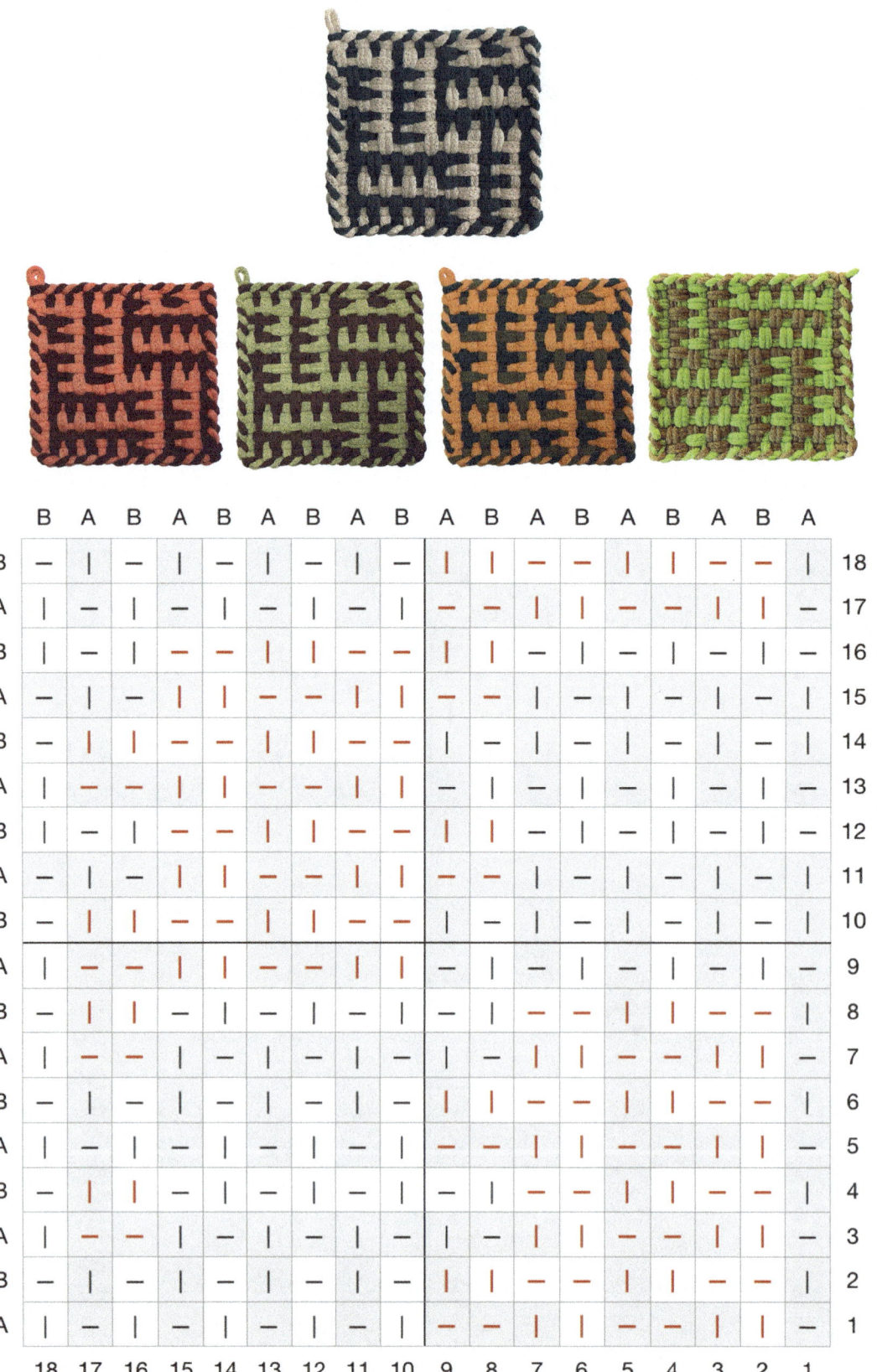

Shadow X
draft from handweaving.net (opgang), charted by Deborah Jean Cohen

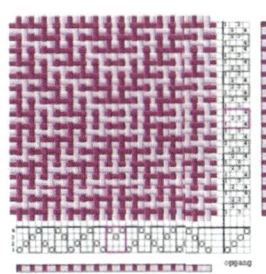

←— The design looks like this if you reverse the weft colors. Here, the warp A is Red and B Carnation. The weft is A Carnation and B Red.

Shadow Zigzag
draft from handweaving.net, charted by Bill West

Vessel III
original design, Bill West

Spider Woman's Cross
draft from handweaving.net, charted by Deborah Jean Cohen

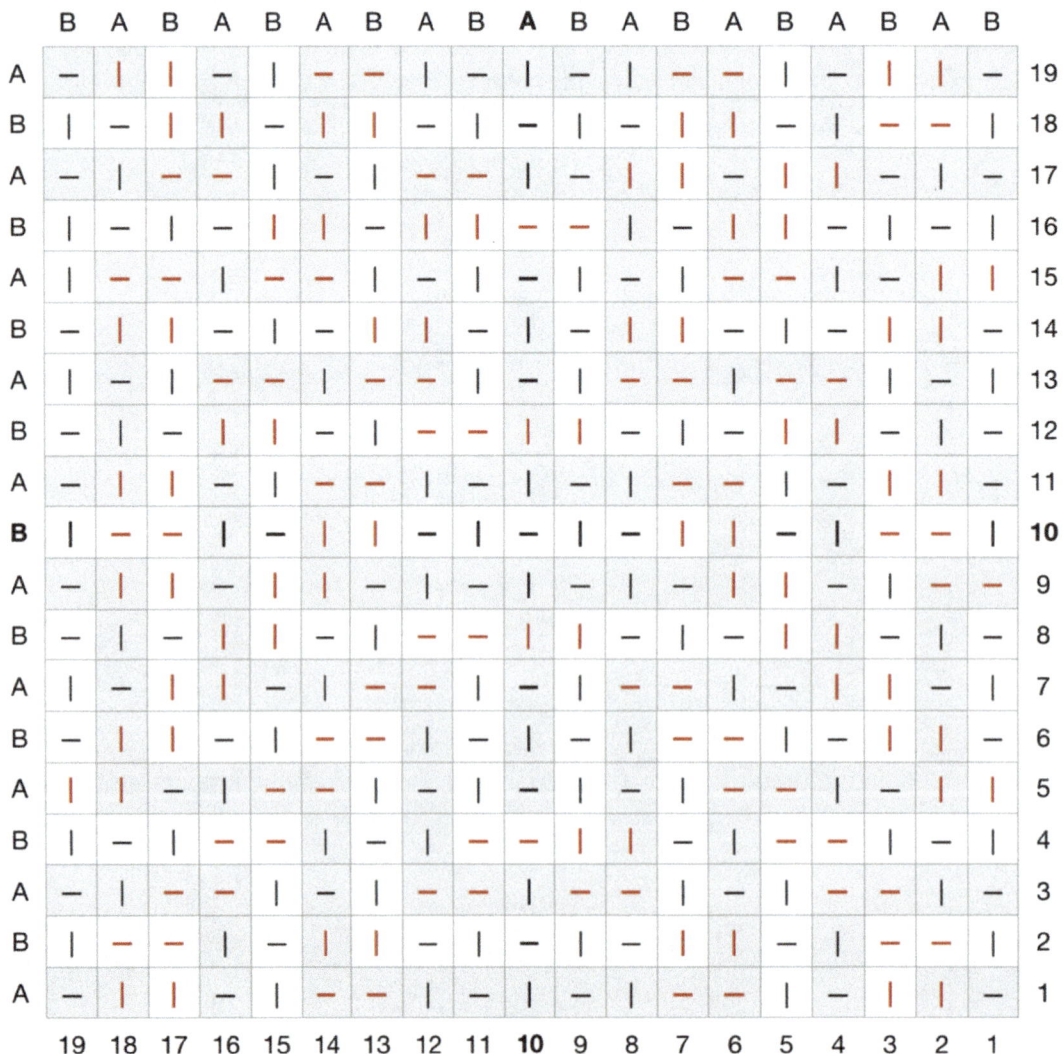

**Spider Woman Cross at the Hubbell auction.
Photo by Mary Walker**

Spider Woman exists in different forms among Southwest Native American nations. To the Navajo Nation, she is Na'ashjélii Asdzáá, and taught the Diné to use wool and weave: but she is much more than that: she was the first to weave the web of the universe.

This is a difficult design to weave, maybe the most difficult of the book. The many 2-floats which accomodate the pattern's angles require loops that have been tugged as much as they'll bear. Radical blocking helps (wet your weave thoroughly, and leave on the loom to dry overnight) and a mix of Harrisville Designs loops with a sturdier loop (Solmate or Wool Novelty) stabilizes the structure. All of these techniques mitigate the draw-in that naturally occurs when there are 2 or more floats.

113

Square-in-a-Square

	B	A	B	A	B	A	B	A	B	A	B	A	B	A	B	A	B	A	B	
B	−	−			−			−			−			−			−			−			−	−	19
A					−			−			−			−			−			−			−					18
B	−					−			−			−			−			−			−					−	17
A			−					−			−			−			−							−			16
B	−			−					−			−			−					−			−			−	15
A			−			−					−			−					−			−			−			14
B	−			−			−					−					−			−			−			−	13
A			−			−			−									−			−			−			12
B	−			−			−					−			−			−			−			−	11
A			−			−			−			−			−			−			−			−			**10**
B	−			−			−			−	−			−			−			−			−	9
A			−			−									−			−			−			−			8
B	−			−					−					−			−			−			−			−	7
A			−					−			−					−			−			−			−			6
B	−			−				−			−			−					−					−			−	5
A			−							−			−			−							−			4
B	−					−			−			−			−			−							−	3
A					−			−			−			−			−			−							2
B	−	−			−			−			−			−			−			−			−	−	1
	19	18	17	16	15	14	13	12	11	**10**	9	8	7	6	5	4	3	2	1	

Square-in-a-Square isn't symmetrical on an 18-peg loom, but can be woven symmetrically on that loom using only 17 pegs. This is a 17-pegger woven in Harrisville Designs Chocolate, Ochre, Autumn, and Flax.

115

Straight-edged Spiral
original design, Mary Clarke

Wavy Zigzag, Top Left
draft from handweaving.com, charted by Bill West

Wavy Zigzag, Top Right
draft from handweaving.com, charted by Bill West

Wavy Zigzag, Bottom Left
draft from handweaving.com, charted by Bill West

Wavy Zigzag, Bottom Right
draft from handweaving.com, charted by Bill West

Square Maze

original design, Bill West

<table>
<tr><th></th><th>B</th><th>A</th><th>B</th><th>A</th><th>B</th><th>A</th><th>B</th><th>A</th><th>B</th><th>A</th><th>B</th><th>A</th><th>B</th><th>**A**</th><th>B</th><th>A</th><th>B</th><th>A</th><th>B</th><th>A</th><th>B</th><th>A</th><th>B</th><th>A</th><th>B</th><th>A</th><th>B</th><th></th></tr>
<tr><td>B</td><td>—</td><td>—</td><td>|</td><td>—</td><td>|</td><td>—</td><td>|</td><td>—</td><td>|</td><td>—</td><td>|</td><td>—</td><td>|</td><td>—</td><td>|</td><td>—</td><td>|</td><td>—</td><td>|</td><td>—</td><td>|</td><td>—</td><td>|</td><td>—</td><td>|</td><td>—</td><td>—</td><td>27</td></tr>
<tr><td>A</td><td>|</td><td>—</td><td>—</td><td>|</td><td>—</td><td>|</td><td>—</td><td>|</td><td>—</td><td>|</td><td>—</td><td>|</td><td>—</td><td>|</td><td>—</td><td>|</td><td>—</td><td>|</td><td>—</td><td>|</td><td>—</td><td>|</td><td>—</td><td>|</td><td>—</td><td>—</td><td>|</td><td>26</td></tr>
<tr><td>B</td><td>—</td><td>|</td><td>—</td><td>—</td><td>|</td><td>—</td><td>|</td><td>—</td><td>|</td><td>—</td><td>|</td><td>—</td><td>|</td><td>—</td><td>|</td><td>—</td><td>|</td><td>—</td><td>|</td><td>—</td><td>|</td><td>—</td><td>|</td><td>—</td><td>—</td><td>|</td><td>—</td><td>25</td></tr>
<tr><td>A</td><td>|</td><td>—</td><td>|</td><td>—</td><td>—</td><td>|</td><td>—</td><td>|</td><td>—</td><td>|</td><td>—</td><td>|</td><td>—</td><td>|</td><td>—</td><td>|</td><td>—</td><td>|</td><td>—</td><td>|</td><td>—</td><td>|</td><td>—</td><td>—</td><td>|</td><td>—</td><td>|</td><td>24</td></tr>
<tr><td>B</td><td>—</td><td>|</td><td>—</td><td>|</td><td>—</td><td>—</td><td>|</td><td>—</td><td>|</td><td>—</td><td>|</td><td>—</td><td>|</td><td>—</td><td>|</td><td>—</td><td>|</td><td>—</td><td>|</td><td>—</td><td>|</td><td>—</td><td>—</td><td>|</td><td>—</td><td>|</td><td>—</td><td>23</td></tr>
<tr><td>A</td><td>|</td><td>—</td><td>|</td><td>—</td><td>|</td><td>—</td><td>—</td><td>|</td><td>—</td><td>|</td><td>—</td><td>|</td><td>—</td><td>|</td><td>—</td><td>|</td><td>—</td><td>|</td><td>—</td><td>|</td><td>—</td><td>—</td><td>|</td><td>—</td><td>|</td><td>—</td><td>|</td><td>22</td></tr>
<tr><td>B</td><td>—</td><td>|</td><td>—</td><td>|</td><td>—</td><td>|</td><td>—</td><td>—</td><td>|</td><td>—</td><td>|</td><td>—</td><td>|</td><td>—</td><td>|</td><td>—</td><td>|</td><td>—</td><td>|</td><td>—</td><td>—</td><td>|</td><td>—</td><td>|</td><td>—</td><td>|</td><td>—</td><td>21</td></tr>
<tr><td>A</td><td>|</td><td>—</td><td>|</td><td>—</td><td>|</td><td>—</td><td>|</td><td>—</td><td>—</td><td>|</td><td>—</td><td>|</td><td>—</td><td>|</td><td>—</td><td>|</td><td>—</td><td>|</td><td>—</td><td>—</td><td>|</td><td>—</td><td>|</td><td>—</td><td>|</td><td>—</td><td>|</td><td>20</td></tr>
<tr><td>B</td><td>—</td><td>|</td><td>—</td><td>|</td><td>—</td><td>|</td><td>—</td><td>|</td><td>—</td><td>—</td><td>|</td><td>—</td><td>|</td><td>—</td><td>|</td><td>—</td><td>|</td><td>—</td><td>—</td><td>|</td><td>—</td><td>|</td><td>—</td><td>|</td><td>—</td><td>|</td><td>—</td><td>19</td></tr>
<tr><td>A</td><td>|</td><td>—</td><td>|</td><td>—</td><td>|</td><td>—</td><td>|</td><td>—</td><td>|</td><td>—</td><td>—</td><td>|</td><td>—</td><td>|</td><td>—</td><td>|</td><td>—</td><td>—</td><td>|</td><td>—</td><td>|</td><td>—</td><td>|</td><td>—</td><td>|</td><td>—</td><td>|</td><td>18</td></tr>
<tr><td>B</td><td>—</td><td>|</td><td>—</td><td>|</td><td>—</td><td>|</td><td>—</td><td>|</td><td>—</td><td>|</td><td>—</td><td>—</td><td>|</td><td>—</td><td>|</td><td>—</td><td>—</td><td>|</td><td>—</td><td>|</td><td>—</td><td>|</td><td>—</td><td>|</td><td>—</td><td>|</td><td>—</td><td>17</td></tr>
<tr><td>A</td><td>|</td><td>—</td><td>|</td><td>—</td><td>|</td><td>—</td><td>|</td><td>—</td><td>|</td><td>—</td><td>|</td><td>—</td><td>—</td><td>|</td><td>—</td><td>—</td><td>|</td><td>—</td><td>|</td><td>—</td><td>|</td><td>—</td><td>|</td><td>—</td><td>|</td><td>—</td><td>|</td><td>16</td></tr>
<tr><td>B</td><td>—</td><td>|</td><td>—</td><td>|</td><td>—</td><td>|</td><td>—</td><td>|</td><td>—</td><td>|</td><td>—</td><td>|</td><td>|</td><td>—</td><td>—</td><td>|</td><td>—</td><td>|</td><td>—</td><td>|</td><td>—</td><td>|</td><td>—</td><td>|</td><td>—</td><td>|</td><td>—</td><td>15</td></tr>
<tr><td>**A**</td><td>|</td><td>—</td><td>|</td><td>—</td><td>|</td><td>—</td><td>|</td><td>—</td><td>|</td><td>—</td><td>|</td><td>|</td><td>—</td><td>|</td><td>|</td><td>—</td><td>|</td><td>—</td><td>|</td><td>—</td><td>|</td><td>—</td><td>|</td><td>—</td><td>|</td><td>—</td><td>|</td><td>**14**</td></tr>
<tr><td>B</td><td>—</td><td>|</td><td>—</td><td>|</td><td>—</td><td>|</td><td>—</td><td>|</td><td>—</td><td>|</td><td>—</td><td>—</td><td>|</td><td>—</td><td>—</td><td>|</td><td>—</td><td>|</td><td>—</td><td>|</td><td>—</td><td>|</td><td>—</td><td>|</td><td>—</td><td>|</td><td>—</td><td>13</td></tr>
<tr><td>A</td><td>|</td><td>—</td><td>|</td><td>—</td><td>|</td><td>—</td><td>|</td><td>—</td><td>|</td><td>—</td><td>—</td><td>|</td><td>—</td><td>|</td><td>—</td><td>—</td><td>|</td><td>—</td><td>|</td><td>—</td><td>|</td><td>—</td><td>|</td><td>—</td><td>|</td><td>—</td><td>|</td><td>12</td></tr>
<tr><td>B</td><td>—</td><td>|</td><td>—</td><td>|</td><td>—</td><td>|</td><td>—</td><td>|</td><td>—</td><td>—</td><td>|</td><td>—</td><td>|</td><td>—</td><td>|</td><td>—</td><td>—</td><td>|</td><td>—</td><td>|</td><td>—</td><td>|</td><td>—</td><td>|</td><td>—</td><td>|</td><td>—</td><td>11</td></tr>
<tr><td>A</td><td>|</td><td>—</td><td>|</td><td>—</td><td>|</td><td>—</td><td>|</td><td>—</td><td>—</td><td>|</td><td>—</td><td>|</td><td>—</td><td>|</td><td>—</td><td>|</td><td>—</td><td>—</td><td>|</td><td>—</td><td>|</td><td>—</td><td>|</td><td>—</td><td>|</td><td>—</td><td>|</td><td>10</td></tr>
<tr><td>B</td><td>—</td><td>|</td><td>—</td><td>|</td><td>—</td><td>|</td><td>—</td><td>—</td><td>|</td><td>—</td><td>|</td><td>—</td><td>|</td><td>—</td><td>|</td><td>—</td><td>|</td><td>—</td><td>—</td><td>|</td><td>—</td><td>|</td><td>—</td><td>|</td><td>—</td><td>|</td><td>—</td><td>9</td></tr>
<tr><td>A</td><td>|</td><td>—</td><td>|</td><td>—</td><td>|</td><td>—</td><td>—</td><td>|</td><td>—</td><td>|</td><td>—</td><td>|</td><td>—</td><td>|</td><td>—</td><td>|</td><td>—</td><td>|</td><td>—</td><td>—</td><td>|</td><td>—</td><td>|</td><td>—</td><td>|</td><td>—</td><td>|</td><td>8</td></tr>
<tr><td>B</td><td>—</td><td>|</td><td>—</td><td>|</td><td>—</td><td>—</td><td>|</td><td>—</td><td>|</td><td>—</td><td>|</td><td>—</td><td>|</td><td>—</td><td>|</td><td>—</td><td>|</td><td>—</td><td>|</td><td>—</td><td>—</td><td>|</td><td>—</td><td>|</td><td>—</td><td>|</td><td>—</td><td>7</td></tr>
<tr><td>A</td><td>|</td><td>—</td><td>|</td><td>—</td><td>—</td><td>|</td><td>—</td><td>|</td><td>—</td><td>|</td><td>—</td><td>|</td><td>—</td><td>|</td><td>—</td><td>|</td><td>—</td><td>|</td><td>—</td><td>|</td><td>—</td><td>—</td><td>|</td><td>—</td><td>|</td><td>—</td><td>|</td><td>6</td></tr>
<tr><td>B</td><td>—</td><td>|</td><td>—</td><td>—</td><td>|</td><td>—</td><td>|</td><td>—</td><td>|</td><td>—</td><td>|</td><td>—</td><td>|</td><td>—</td><td>|</td><td>—</td><td>|</td><td>—</td><td>|</td><td>—</td><td>|</td><td>—</td><td>—</td><td>|</td><td>—</td><td>|</td><td>—</td><td>5</td></tr>
<tr><td>A</td><td>|</td><td>|</td><td>—</td><td>|</td><td>—</td><td>|</td><td>—</td><td>|</td><td>—</td><td>|</td><td>—</td><td>|</td><td>—</td><td>|</td><td>—</td><td>|</td><td>—</td><td>|</td><td>—</td><td>|</td><td>—</td><td>|</td><td>—</td><td>—</td><td>|</td><td>—</td><td>|</td><td>4</td></tr>
<tr><td>B</td><td>|</td><td>—</td><td>|</td><td>—</td><td>|</td><td>—</td><td>|</td><td>—</td><td>|</td><td>—</td><td>|</td><td>—</td><td>|</td><td>—</td><td>|</td><td>—</td><td>|</td><td>—</td><td>|</td><td>—</td><td>|</td><td>—</td><td>|</td><td>—</td><td>—</td><td>|</td><td>—</td><td>3</td></tr>
<tr><td>A</td><td>—</td><td>|</td><td>—</td><td>|</td><td>—</td><td>|</td><td>—</td><td>|</td><td>—</td><td>|</td><td>—</td><td>|</td><td>—</td><td>|</td><td>—</td><td>|</td><td>—</td><td>|</td><td>—</td><td>|</td><td>—</td><td>|</td><td>—</td><td>|</td><td>—</td><td>—</td><td>|</td><td>2</td></tr>
<tr><td>B</td><td>—</td><td>—</td><td>|</td><td>—</td><td>|</td><td>—</td><td>|</td><td>—</td><td>|</td><td>—</td><td>|</td><td>—</td><td>|</td><td>—</td><td>|</td><td>—</td><td>|</td><td>—</td><td>|</td><td>—</td><td>|</td><td>—</td><td>|</td><td>—</td><td>|</td><td>—</td><td>—</td><td>1</td></tr>
<tr><td></td><td>27</td><td>26</td><td>25</td><td>24</td><td>23</td><td>22</td><td>21</td><td>20</td><td>19</td><td>18</td><td>17</td><td>16</td><td>15</td><td>**14**</td><td>13</td><td>12</td><td>11</td><td>10</td><td>9</td><td>8</td><td>7</td><td>6</td><td>5</td><td>4</td><td>3</td><td>2</td><td>1</td><td></td></tr>
</table>

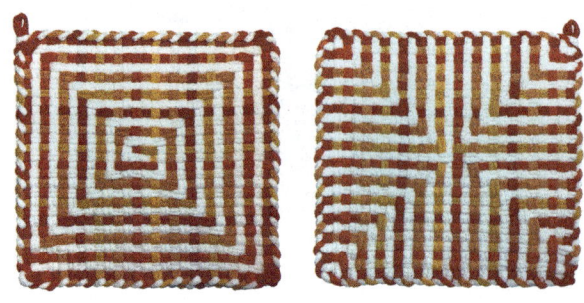

CHAPTER 5
potholder patterns: twill

Twill is a weaving structure where the weft passes over or under one or more threads, then over or under two or more threads, and so on, with an offset between rows. This creates the distinguishing diagonal look of twill that you can see in your denim blue jeans. Blue jeans are also an example of a basic twill, where the warp is one color (in blue jeans, white) and the weft another (in blue jeans, indigo). Check out your frayed jeans!

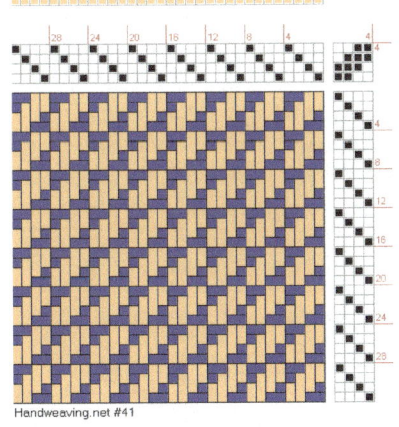

A twill draft.

Because of the floats, twill will draw in more than plain weave and form a denser, stronger fabric: a reason why denim, a sturdy working fabric, is woven in this way. This characteristic also means that a twill potholder will be thicker and smaller than its plain weave counterpart woven on the same loom.

Twill weave is at least 5,000 years old. Minoan Crete frescoes of the Bronze Age (3,000 BCE — 1,500 BCE) showed women wearing various textile patterns, including all-over patterns resembling twills and rosepath twills. (Please reference EJW Barber's "Prehistoric Textiles": a fascinating article.)

Spiral Maze
draft from handweaving.net, charted by Deborah Jean Cohen

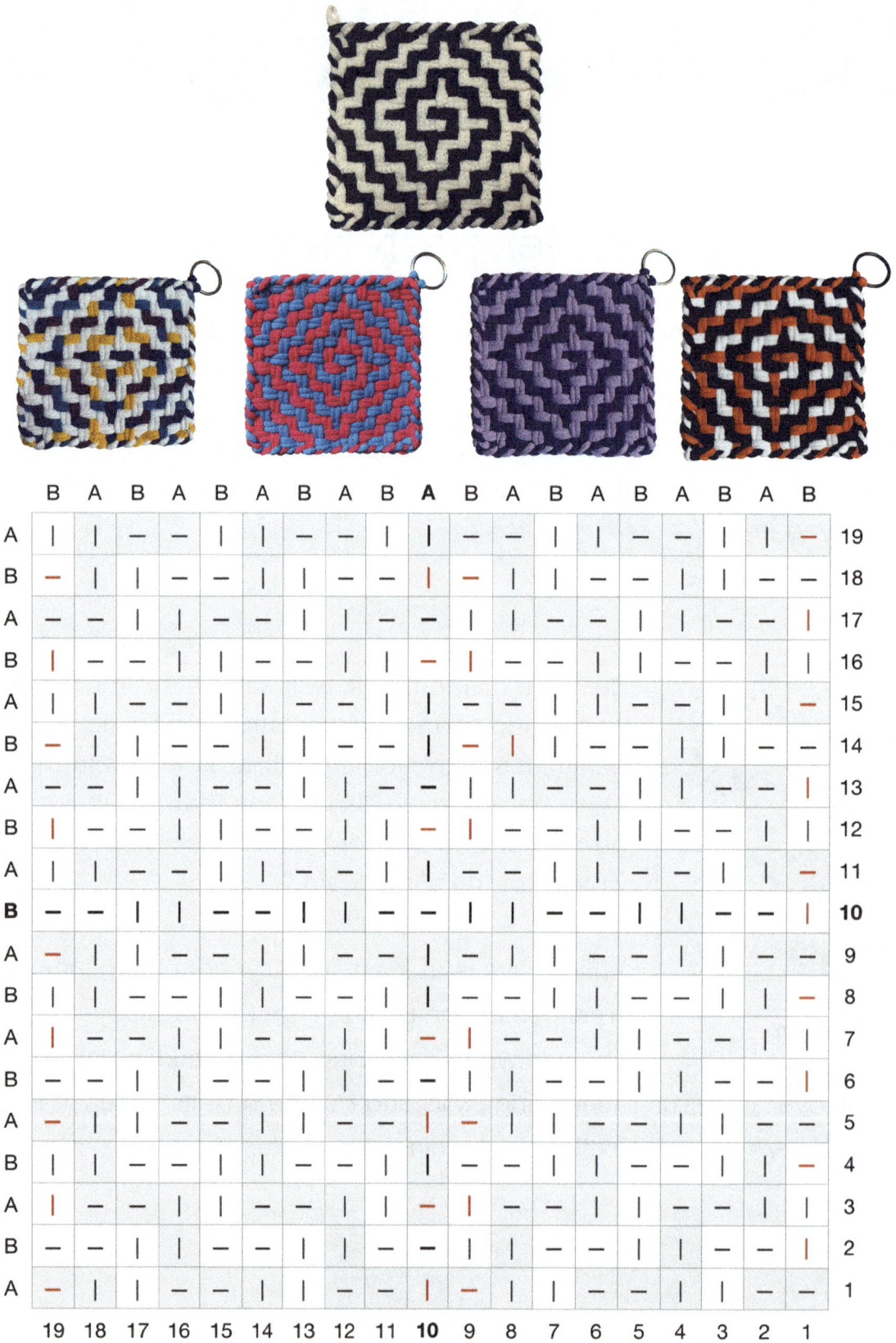

Birds Flying High

Angela West discovered this when she accidentally reversed the weft colors when weaving Exposed Filmstrips. Try it!

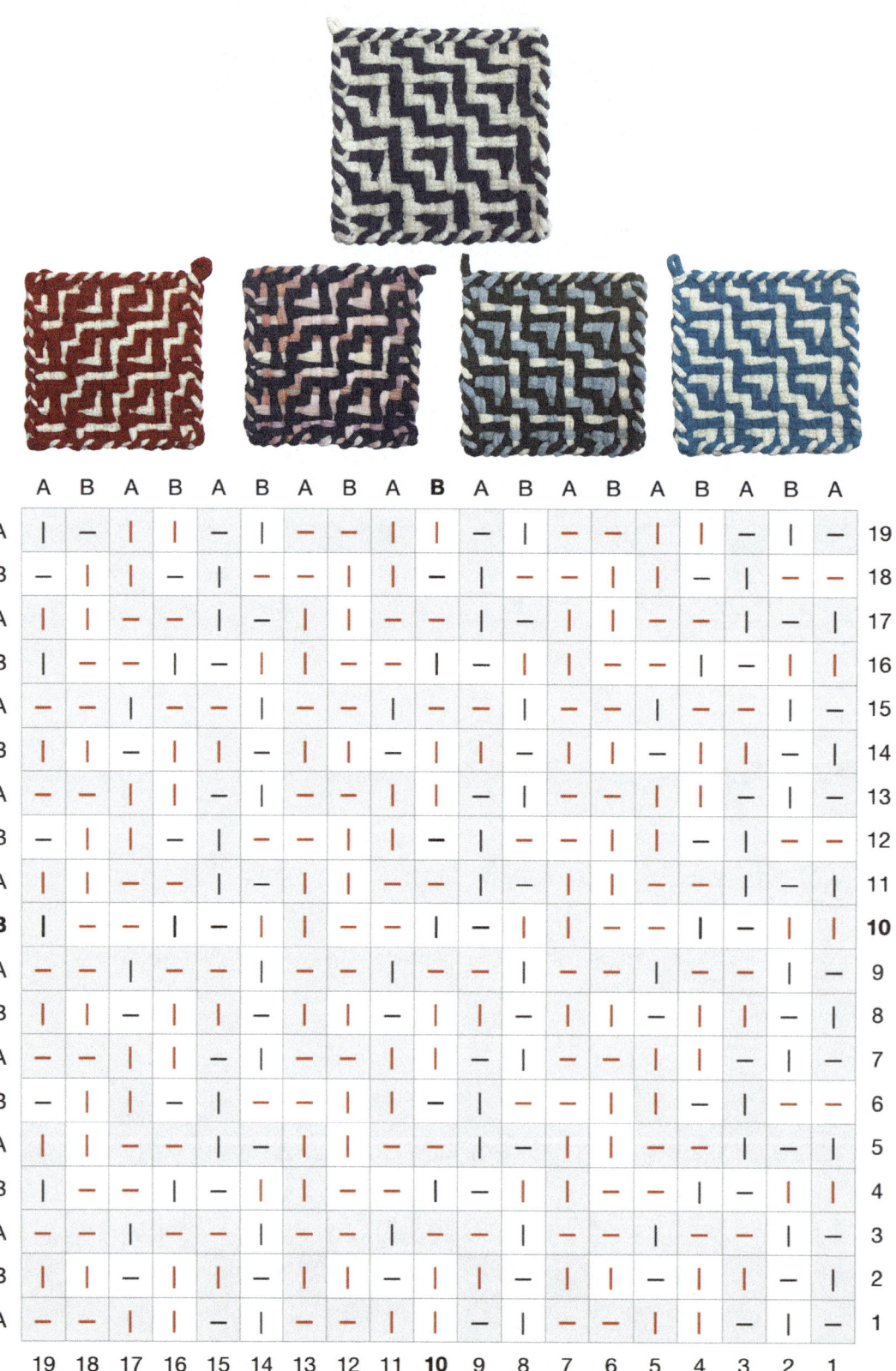

Diamond Burst
draft from handweaving.net, charted by Deborah Jean Cohen
Weave under gray squares. Weave over white squares.

Prism Twill
draft from handweaving.net, charted by Deborah Jean Cohen
Weave under gray squares. Weave over white squares.

Diamond Mix
draft from handweaving.net, charted by Christine Olsen Reis
Weave under gray squares. Weave over white squares.

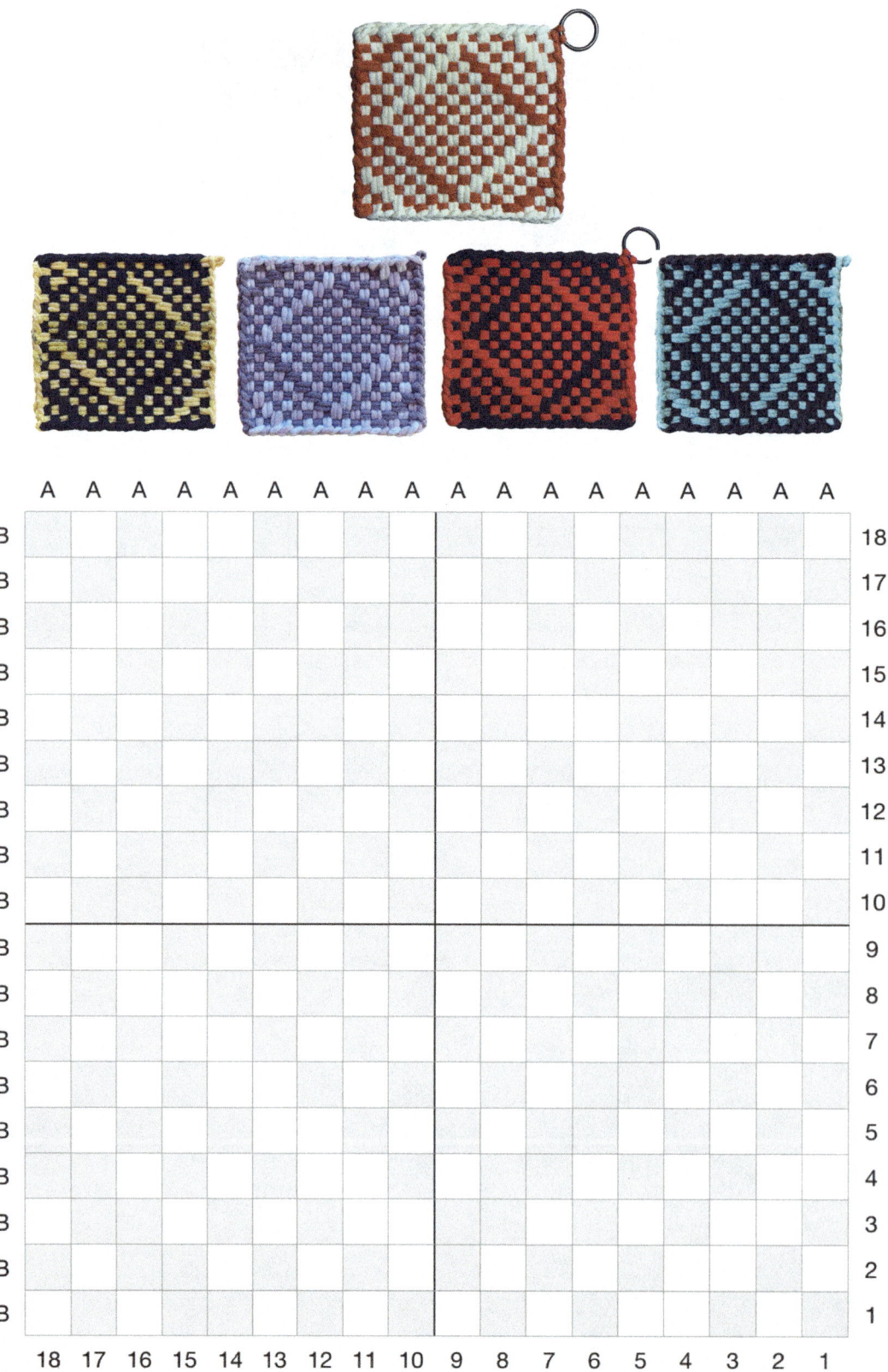

Front and back are the same!

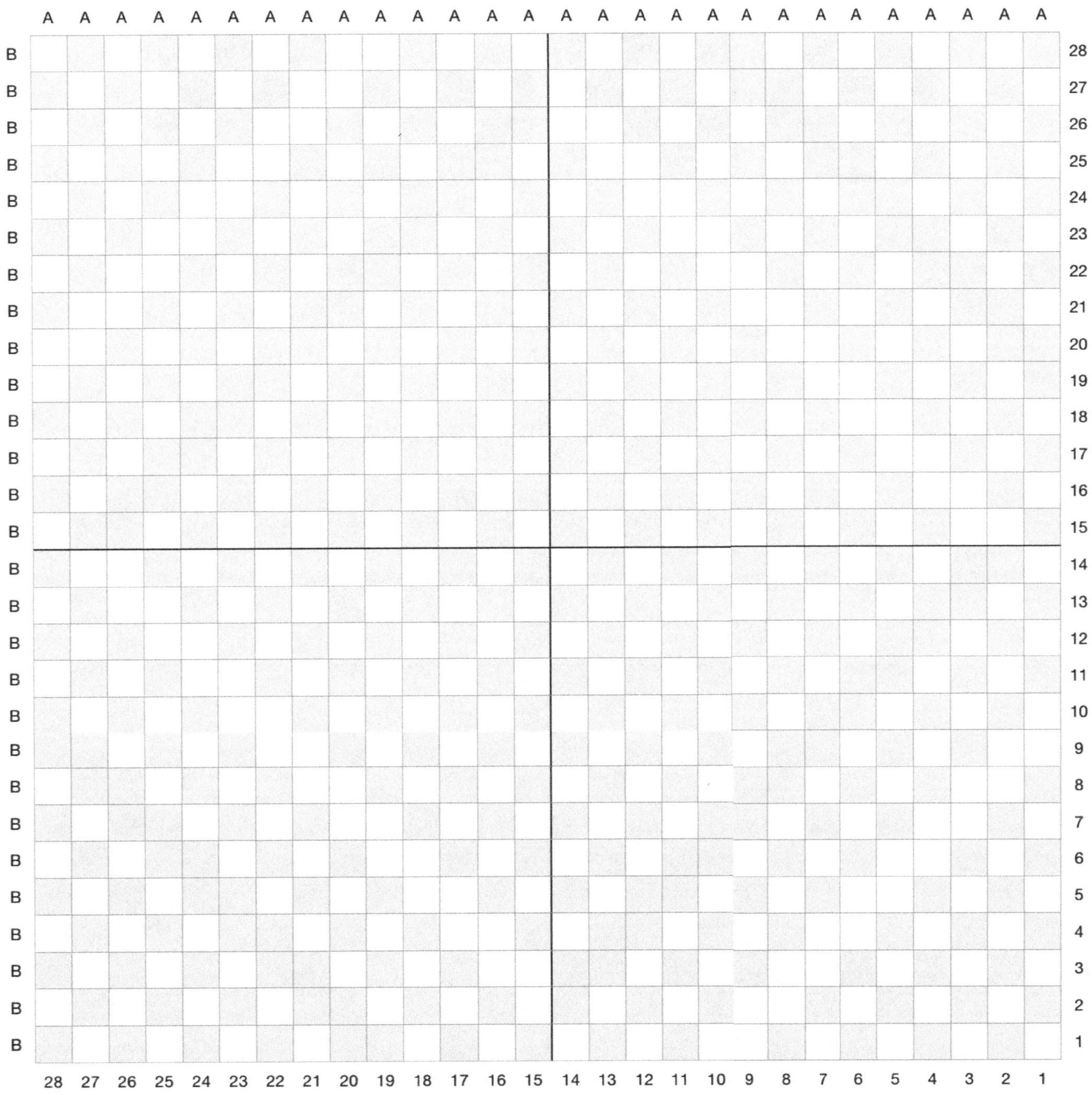

Diamond Repeat
draft from handweaving.net, charted by Deborah Jean Cohen
Weave under gray squares. Weave over white squares.

132

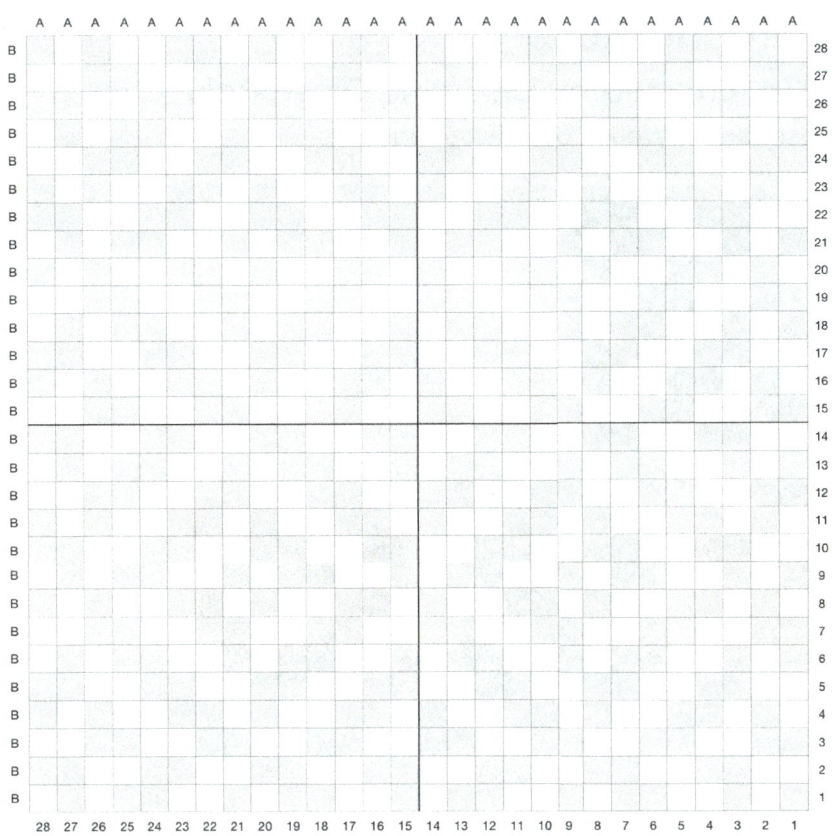

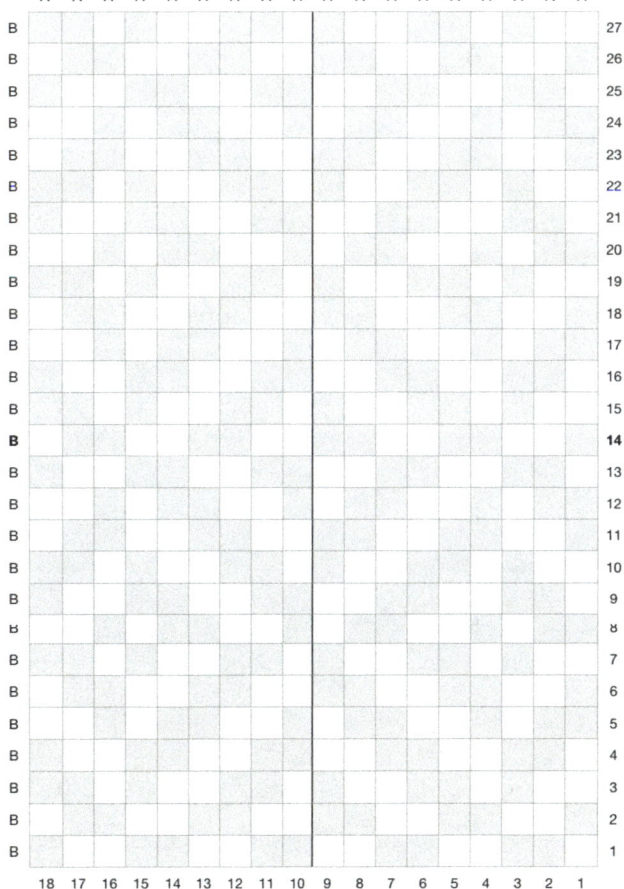

Diamond Rose
handweaving.net #4174, charted by Christine Olsen Reis
Weave under gray squares. Weave over white squares.

	A	A	A	A	A	A	A	A	A	A	A	A	A	**A**	A	A	A	A	A	A	A	A	A	A	A	A	A	
B																												27
B																												26
B																												25
B																												24
B																												23
B																												22
B																												21
B																												20
B																												19
B																												18
B																												17
B																												16
B																												15
B																												**14**
B																												13
B																												12
B																												11
B																												10
B																												9
B																												8
B																												7
B																												6
B																												5
B																												4
B																												3
B																												2
B																												1
	27	26	25	24	23	22	21	20	19	18	17	16	15	**14**	13	12	11	10	9	8	7	6	5	4	3	2	1	

Diamond Twill

Weave under gray squares. Weave over white squares.

Diamonds Are Forever
original design, Bill West
Weave under gray squares. Weave over white squares.

	B	B	B	B	B	B	B	B	B	B	B	B	B	**B**	B	B	B	B	B	B	B	B	B	B	B	B	B	
A																												27
A																												26
A																												25
A																												24
A																												23
A																												22
A																												21
A																												20
A																												19
A																												18
A																												17
A																												16
A																												15
A																												**14**
A																												13
A																												12
A																												11
A																												10
A																												9
A																												8
A																												7
A																												6
A																												5
A																												4
A																												3
A																												2
A																												1
	27	26	25	24	23	22	21	20	19	18	17	16	15	**14**	13	12	11	10	9	8	7	6	5	4	3	2	1	

Exposed Filmstrips
draft from handweaving.net, charted by Bill West

Garden Path
draft from handweaving.net, charted by Bill West

Little Squares/Thor's Hammer
original design, Bill West

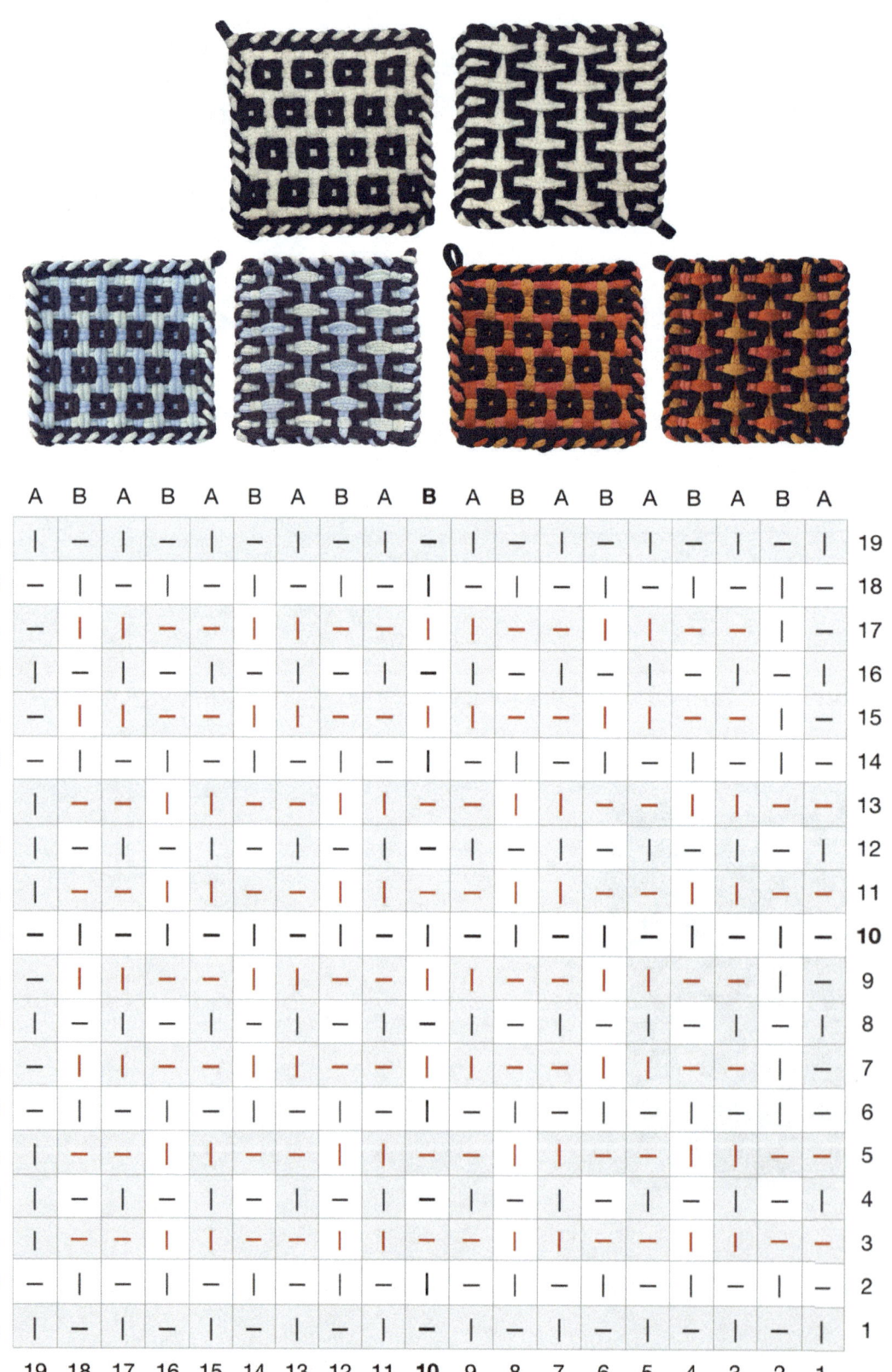

Scattered Twill (Broken Twill)

Weave under gray squares. Weave over white squares.

Up the Down Staircase
original design, Bill West

Shine Bright Like A Diamond
original design, Bill West
Weave under gray squares. Weave over white squares.

B B B B B B B B B B B B B B B B B B B B B B B B B B B
A A A A A A A A A A A A A A A A A A A A A A A A A A A
27 26 25 24 23 22 21 20 19 18 17 16 15 14 13 12 11 10 9 8 7 6 5 4 3 2 1

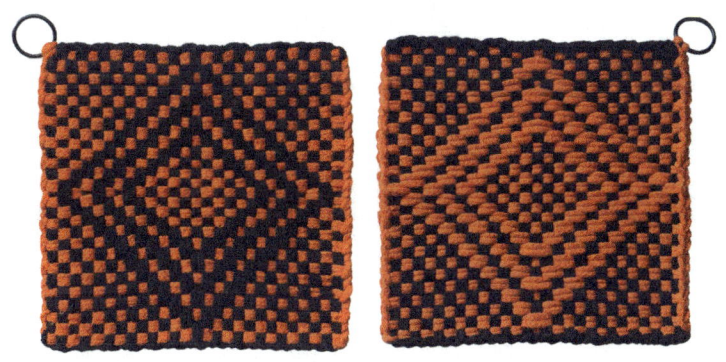

Shuriken
draft from handweaving.net, charted by Deborah Jean Cohen

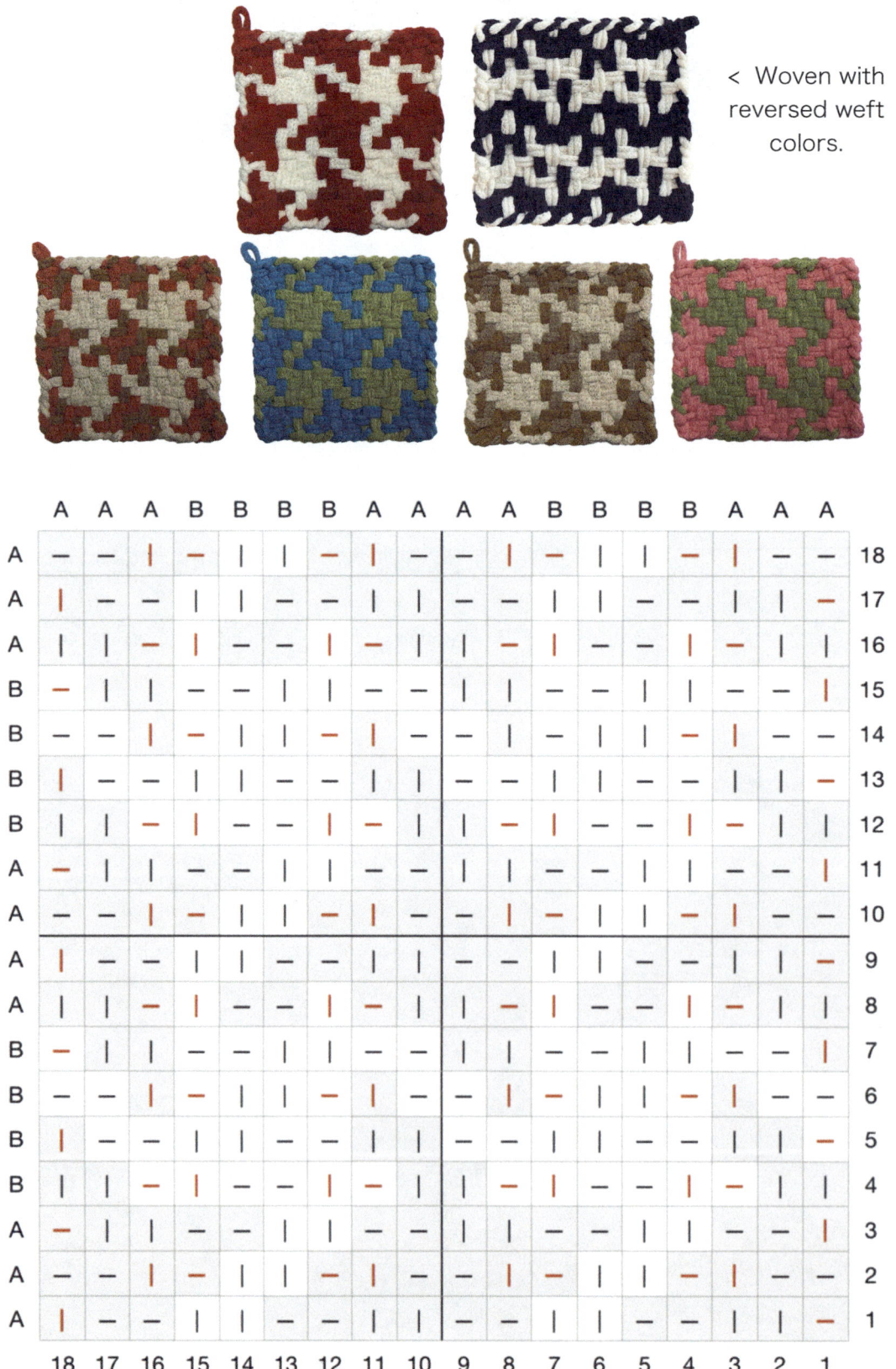

< Woven with reversed weft colors.

Twill X
draft from dixieweaver.com, charted by Deborah Jean Cohen
Weave under gray squares. Weave over white squares.

Wavy Chevron Twill

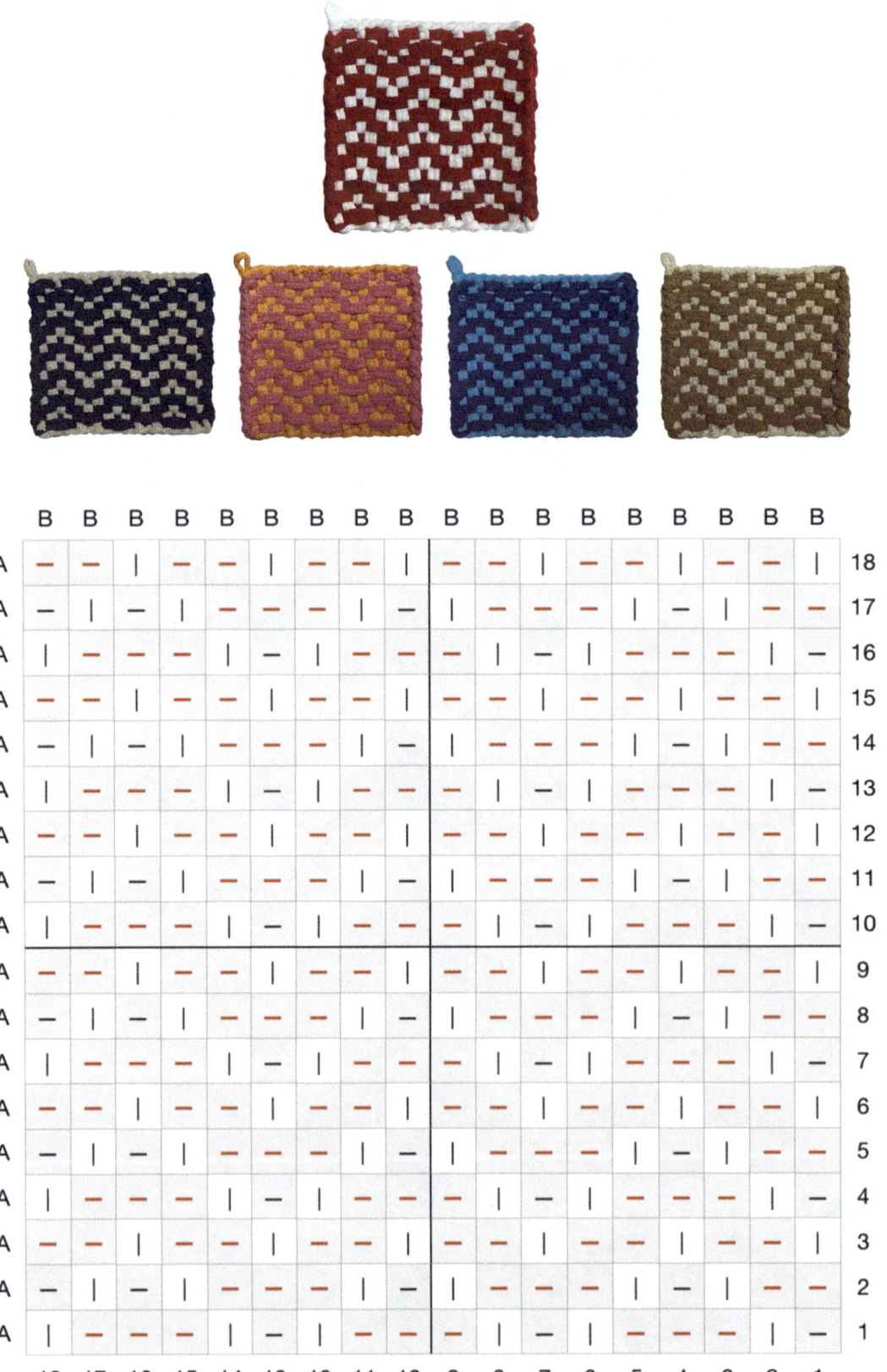

<table>
<tr><td></td><td>B</td><td>B</td><td>B</td><td>B</td><td>B</td><td>B</td><td>B</td><td>B</td><td>B</td><td>B</td><td>B</td><td>B</td><td>B</td><td>B</td><td>B</td><td>B</td><td>B</td><td>B</td><td>B</td><td>B</td><td>B</td><td>B</td><td>B</td><td>B</td><td>B</td><td>B</td><td>B</td><td></td></tr>
<tr><td>A</td><td>–</td><td>|</td><td>–</td><td>|</td><td>–</td><td>–</td><td>–</td><td>|</td><td>–</td><td>|</td><td>–</td><td>–</td><td>–</td><td>|</td><td>–</td><td>|</td><td>–</td><td>–</td><td>–</td><td>|</td><td>–</td><td>|</td><td>–</td><td>–</td><td>–</td><td>|</td><td>–</td><td>27</td></tr>
<tr><td>A</td><td>–</td><td>–</td><td>|</td><td>–</td><td>–</td><td>|</td><td>–</td><td>–</td><td>|</td><td>–</td><td>–</td><td>|</td><td>–</td><td>–</td><td>|</td><td>–</td><td>–</td><td>|</td><td>–</td><td>–</td><td>|</td><td>–</td><td>–</td><td>|</td><td>–</td><td>–</td><td>|</td><td>26</td></tr>
<tr><td>A</td><td>|</td><td>–</td><td>–</td><td>–</td><td>|</td><td>–</td><td>|</td><td>–</td><td>–</td><td>–</td><td>|</td><td>–</td><td>|</td><td>–</td><td>–</td><td>–</td><td>|</td><td>–</td><td>|</td><td>–</td><td>–</td><td>–</td><td>|</td><td>–</td><td>|</td><td>–</td><td>–</td><td>25</td></tr>
<tr><td>A</td><td>–</td><td>|</td><td>–</td><td>|</td><td>–</td><td>–</td><td>–</td><td>|</td><td>–</td><td>|</td><td>–</td><td>–</td><td>–</td><td>|</td><td>–</td><td>|</td><td>–</td><td>–</td><td>–</td><td>|</td><td>–</td><td>|</td><td>–</td><td>–</td><td>–</td><td>|</td><td>–</td><td>24</td></tr>
<tr><td>A</td><td>–</td><td>–</td><td>|</td><td>–</td><td>–</td><td>|</td><td>–</td><td>–</td><td>|</td><td>–</td><td>–</td><td>|</td><td>–</td><td>–</td><td>|</td><td>–</td><td>–</td><td>|</td><td>–</td><td>–</td><td>|</td><td>–</td><td>–</td><td>|</td><td>–</td><td>–</td><td>|</td><td>23</td></tr>
<tr><td>A</td><td>|</td><td>–</td><td>–</td><td>–</td><td>|</td><td>–</td><td>|</td><td>–</td><td>–</td><td>–</td><td>|</td><td>–</td><td>|</td><td>–</td><td>–</td><td>–</td><td>|</td><td>–</td><td>|</td><td>–</td><td>–</td><td>–</td><td>|</td><td>–</td><td>|</td><td>–</td><td>–</td><td>22</td></tr>
<tr><td>A</td><td>–</td><td>|</td><td>–</td><td>|</td><td>–</td><td>–</td><td>–</td><td>|</td><td>–</td><td>|</td><td>–</td><td>–</td><td>–</td><td>|</td><td>–</td><td>|</td><td>–</td><td>–</td><td>–</td><td>|</td><td>–</td><td>|</td><td>–</td><td>–</td><td>–</td><td>|</td><td>–</td><td>21</td></tr>
<tr><td>A</td><td>–</td><td>–</td><td>|</td><td>–</td><td>–</td><td>|</td><td>–</td><td>–</td><td>|</td><td>–</td><td>–</td><td>|</td><td>–</td><td>–</td><td>|</td><td>–</td><td>–</td><td>|</td><td>–</td><td>–</td><td>|</td><td>–</td><td>–</td><td>|</td><td>–</td><td>–</td><td>|</td><td>20</td></tr>
<tr><td>A</td><td>|</td><td>–</td><td>–</td><td>–</td><td>|</td><td>–</td><td>|</td><td>–</td><td>–</td><td>–</td><td>|</td><td>–</td><td>|</td><td>–</td><td>–</td><td>–</td><td>|</td><td>–</td><td>|</td><td>–</td><td>–</td><td>–</td><td>|</td><td>–</td><td>|</td><td>–</td><td>–</td><td>19</td></tr>
<tr><td>A</td><td>–</td><td>|</td><td>–</td><td>|</td><td>–</td><td>–</td><td>–</td><td>|</td><td>–</td><td>|</td><td>–</td><td>–</td><td>–</td><td>|</td><td>–</td><td>|</td><td>–</td><td>–</td><td>–</td><td>|</td><td>–</td><td>|</td><td>–</td><td>–</td><td>–</td><td>|</td><td>–</td><td>18</td></tr>
<tr><td>A</td><td>–</td><td>–</td><td>|</td><td>–</td><td>–</td><td>|</td><td>–</td><td>–</td><td>|</td><td>–</td><td>–</td><td>|</td><td>–</td><td>–</td><td>|</td><td>–</td><td>–</td><td>|</td><td>–</td><td>–</td><td>|</td><td>–</td><td>–</td><td>|</td><td>–</td><td>–</td><td>|</td><td>17</td></tr>
<tr><td>A</td><td>|</td><td>–</td><td>–</td><td>–</td><td>|</td><td>–</td><td>|</td><td>–</td><td>–</td><td>–</td><td>|</td><td>–</td><td>|</td><td>–</td><td>–</td><td>–</td><td>|</td><td>–</td><td>|</td><td>–</td><td>–</td><td>–</td><td>|</td><td>–</td><td>|</td><td>–</td><td>–</td><td>16</td></tr>
<tr><td>A</td><td>–</td><td>|</td><td>–</td><td>|</td><td>–</td><td>–</td><td>–</td><td>|</td><td>–</td><td>|</td><td>–</td><td>–</td><td>–</td><td>|</td><td>–</td><td>|</td><td>–</td><td>–</td><td>–</td><td>|</td><td>–</td><td>|</td><td>–</td><td>–</td><td>–</td><td>|</td><td>–</td><td>15</td></tr>
<tr><td>A</td><td>–</td><td>–</td><td>|</td><td>–</td><td>–</td><td>|</td><td>–</td><td>–</td><td>|</td><td>–</td><td>–</td><td>|</td><td>–</td><td>–</td><td>|</td><td>–</td><td>–</td><td>|</td><td>–</td><td>–</td><td>|</td><td>–</td><td>–</td><td>|</td><td>–</td><td>–</td><td>|</td><td>14</td></tr>
<tr><td>A</td><td>|</td><td>–</td><td>–</td><td>–</td><td>|</td><td>–</td><td>|</td><td>–</td><td>–</td><td>–</td><td>|</td><td>–</td><td>|</td><td>–</td><td>–</td><td>–</td><td>|</td><td>–</td><td>|</td><td>–</td><td>–</td><td>–</td><td>|</td><td>–</td><td>|</td><td>–</td><td>–</td><td>13</td></tr>
<tr><td>A</td><td>–</td><td>|</td><td>–</td><td>|</td><td>–</td><td>–</td><td>–</td><td>|</td><td>–</td><td>|</td><td>–</td><td>–</td><td>–</td><td>|</td><td>–</td><td>|</td><td>–</td><td>–</td><td>–</td><td>|</td><td>–</td><td>|</td><td>–</td><td>–</td><td>–</td><td>|</td><td>–</td><td>12</td></tr>
<tr><td>A</td><td>–</td><td>–</td><td>|</td><td>–</td><td>–</td><td>|</td><td>–</td><td>–</td><td>|</td><td>–</td><td>–</td><td>|</td><td>–</td><td>–</td><td>|</td><td>–</td><td>–</td><td>|</td><td>–</td><td>–</td><td>|</td><td>–</td><td>–</td><td>|</td><td>–</td><td>–</td><td>|</td><td>11</td></tr>
<tr><td>A</td><td>|</td><td>–</td><td>–</td><td>–</td><td>|</td><td>–</td><td>|</td><td>–</td><td>–</td><td>–</td><td>|</td><td>–</td><td>|</td><td>–</td><td>–</td><td>–</td><td>|</td><td>–</td><td>|</td><td>–</td><td>–</td><td>–</td><td>|</td><td>–</td><td>|</td><td>–</td><td>–</td><td>10</td></tr>
<tr><td>A</td><td>–</td><td>|</td><td>–</td><td>|</td><td>–</td><td>–</td><td>–</td><td>|</td><td>–</td><td>|</td><td>–</td><td>–</td><td>–</td><td>|</td><td>–</td><td>|</td><td>–</td><td>–</td><td>–</td><td>|</td><td>–</td><td>|</td><td>–</td><td>–</td><td>–</td><td>|</td><td>–</td><td>9</td></tr>
<tr><td>A</td><td>–</td><td>–</td><td>|</td><td>–</td><td>–</td><td>|</td><td>–</td><td>–</td><td>|</td><td>–</td><td>–</td><td>|</td><td>–</td><td>–</td><td>|</td><td>–</td><td>–</td><td>|</td><td>–</td><td>–</td><td>|</td><td>–</td><td>–</td><td>|</td><td>–</td><td>–</td><td>|</td><td>8</td></tr>
<tr><td>A</td><td>|</td><td>–</td><td>–</td><td>–</td><td>|</td><td>–</td><td>|</td><td>–</td><td>–</td><td>–</td><td>|</td><td>–</td><td>|</td><td>–</td><td>–</td><td>–</td><td>|</td><td>–</td><td>|</td><td>–</td><td>–</td><td>–</td><td>|</td><td>–</td><td>|</td><td>–</td><td>–</td><td>7</td></tr>
<tr><td>A</td><td>–</td><td>|</td><td>–</td><td>|</td><td>–</td><td>–</td><td>–</td><td>|</td><td>–</td><td>|</td><td>–</td><td>–</td><td>–</td><td>|</td><td>–</td><td>|</td><td>–</td><td>–</td><td>–</td><td>|</td><td>–</td><td>|</td><td>–</td><td>–</td><td>–</td><td>|</td><td>–</td><td>6</td></tr>
<tr><td>A</td><td>–</td><td>–</td><td>|</td><td>–</td><td>–</td><td>|</td><td>–</td><td>–</td><td>|</td><td>–</td><td>–</td><td>|</td><td>–</td><td>–</td><td>|</td><td>–</td><td>–</td><td>|</td><td>–</td><td>–</td><td>|</td><td>–</td><td>–</td><td>|</td><td>–</td><td>–</td><td>|</td><td>5</td></tr>
<tr><td>A</td><td>|</td><td>–</td><td>–</td><td>–</td><td>|</td><td>–</td><td>|</td><td>–</td><td>–</td><td>–</td><td>|</td><td>–</td><td>|</td><td>–</td><td>–</td><td>–</td><td>|</td><td>–</td><td>|</td><td>–</td><td>–</td><td>–</td><td>|</td><td>–</td><td>|</td><td>–</td><td>–</td><td>4</td></tr>
<tr><td>A</td><td>–</td><td>|</td><td>–</td><td>|</td><td>–</td><td>–</td><td>–</td><td>|</td><td>–</td><td>|</td><td>–</td><td>–</td><td>–</td><td>|</td><td>–</td><td>|</td><td>–</td><td>–</td><td>–</td><td>|</td><td>–</td><td>|</td><td>–</td><td>–</td><td>–</td><td>|</td><td>–</td><td>3</td></tr>
<tr><td>A</td><td>–</td><td>–</td><td>|</td><td>–</td><td>–</td><td>|</td><td>–</td><td>–</td><td>|</td><td>–</td><td>–</td><td>|</td><td>–</td><td>–</td><td>|</td><td>–</td><td>–</td><td>|</td><td>–</td><td>–</td><td>|</td><td>–</td><td>–</td><td>|</td><td>–</td><td>–</td><td>|</td><td>2</td></tr>
<tr><td>A</td><td>|</td><td>–</td><td>–</td><td>–</td><td>|</td><td>–</td><td>|</td><td>–</td><td>–</td><td>–</td><td>|</td><td>–</td><td>|</td><td>–</td><td>–</td><td>–</td><td>|</td><td>–</td><td>|</td><td>–</td><td>–</td><td>–</td><td>|</td><td>–</td><td>|</td><td>–</td><td>–</td><td>1</td></tr>
<tr><td></td><td>27</td><td>26</td><td>25</td><td>24</td><td>23</td><td>22</td><td>21</td><td>20</td><td>19</td><td>18</td><td>17</td><td>16</td><td>15</td><td>14</td><td>13</td><td>12</td><td>11</td><td>10</td><td>9</td><td>8</td><td>7</td><td>6</td><td>5</td><td>4</td><td>3</td><td>2</td><td>1</td><td></td></tr>
</table>

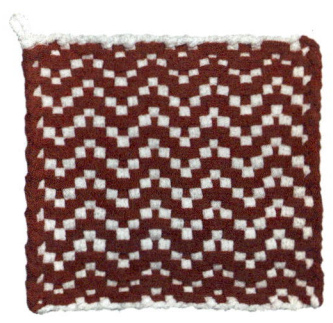

Wiggle Worms
draft from handweaving.net, charted by Bill West

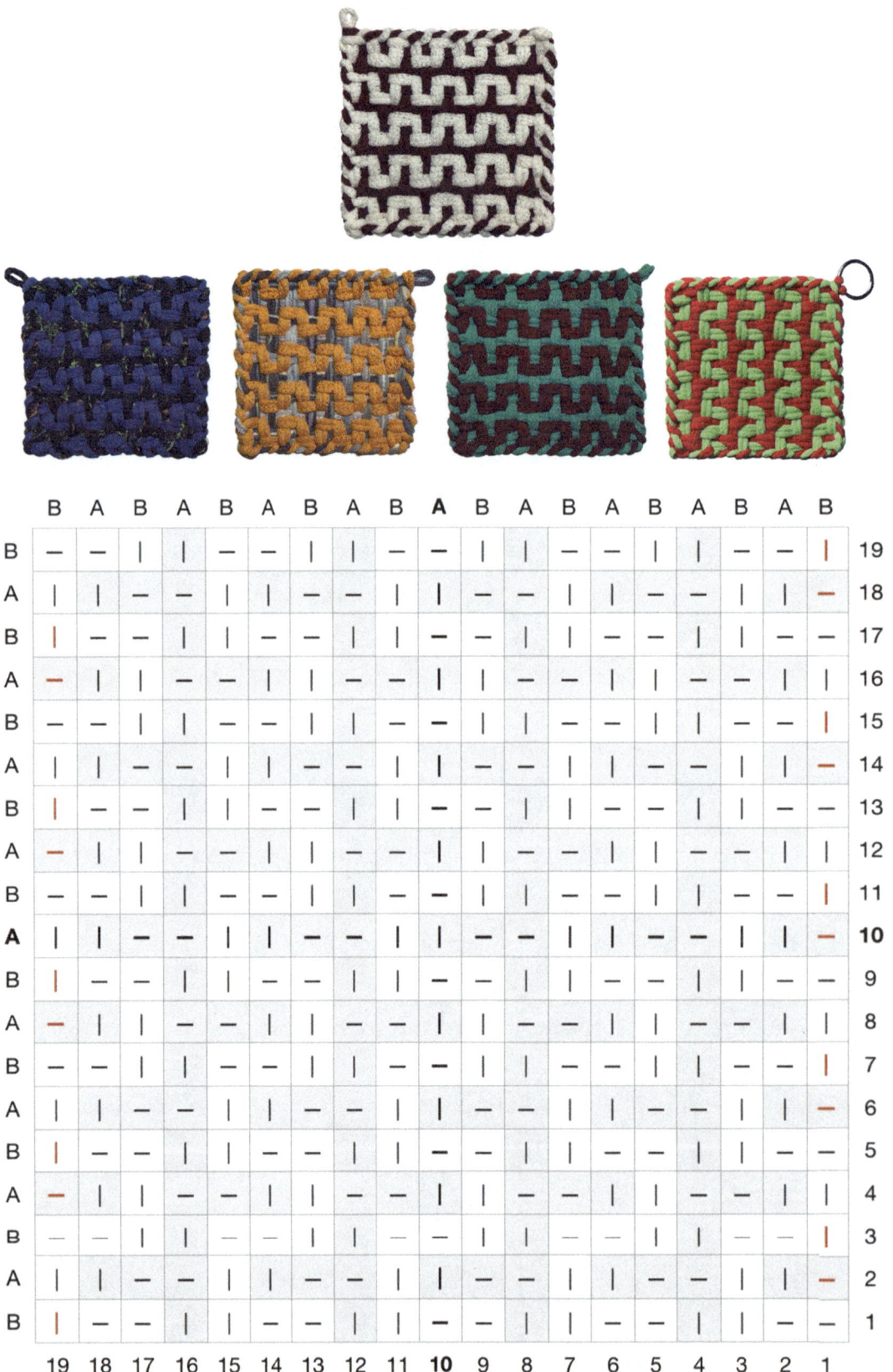

<table>
<tr><th></th><th>B</th><th>A</th><th>B</th><th>A</th><th>B</th><th>A</th><th>B</th><th>A</th><th>B</th><th>A</th><th>B</th><th>A</th><th>B</th><th>A</th><th>B</th><th>A</th><th>B</th><th>A</th><th>B</th><th>A</th><th>B</th><th>A</th><th>B</th><th>A</th><th>B</th><th>A</th><th>B</th><th></th></tr>
<tr><td>B</td><td>—</td><td>—</td><td>|</td><td>|</td><td>—</td><td>—</td><td>|</td><td>|</td><td>—</td><td>—</td><td>|</td><td>|</td><td>—</td><td>—</td><td>|</td><td>|</td><td>—</td><td>—</td><td>|</td><td>|</td><td>—</td><td>—</td><td>|</td><td>|</td><td>—</td><td>—</td><td>|</td><td>27</td></tr>
<tr><td>A</td><td>|</td><td>|</td><td>—</td><td>—</td><td>|</td><td>|</td><td>—</td><td>—</td><td>|</td><td>|</td><td>—</td><td>—</td><td>|</td><td>|</td><td>—</td><td>—</td><td>|</td><td>|</td><td>—</td><td>—</td><td>|</td><td>|</td><td>—</td><td>—</td><td>|</td><td>|</td><td>—</td><td>26</td></tr>
<tr><td>B</td><td>|</td><td>—</td><td>—</td><td>|</td><td>|</td><td>—</td><td>—</td><td>|</td><td>|</td><td>—</td><td>—</td><td>|</td><td>|</td><td>—</td><td>—</td><td>|</td><td>|</td><td>—</td><td>—</td><td>|</td><td>|</td><td>—</td><td>—</td><td>|</td><td>|</td><td>—</td><td>—</td><td>25</td></tr>
<tr><td>A</td><td>—</td><td>|</td><td>|</td><td>—</td><td>—</td><td>|</td><td>|</td><td>—</td><td>—</td><td>|</td><td>|</td><td>—</td><td>—</td><td>|</td><td>|</td><td>—</td><td>—</td><td>|</td><td>|</td><td>—</td><td>—</td><td>|</td><td>|</td><td>—</td><td>—</td><td>|</td><td>|</td><td>24</td></tr>
<tr><td>B</td><td>—</td><td>—</td><td>|</td><td>|</td><td>—</td><td>—</td><td>|</td><td>|</td><td>—</td><td>—</td><td>|</td><td>|</td><td>—</td><td>—</td><td>|</td><td>|</td><td>—</td><td>—</td><td>|</td><td>|</td><td>—</td><td>—</td><td>|</td><td>|</td><td>—</td><td>—</td><td>|</td><td>23</td></tr>
<tr><td>A</td><td>|</td><td>|</td><td>—</td><td>—</td><td>|</td><td>|</td><td>—</td><td>—</td><td>|</td><td>|</td><td>—</td><td>—</td><td>|</td><td>|</td><td>—</td><td>—</td><td>|</td><td>|</td><td>—</td><td>—</td><td>|</td><td>|</td><td>—</td><td>—</td><td>|</td><td>|</td><td>—</td><td>22</td></tr>
<tr><td>B</td><td>|</td><td>—</td><td>—</td><td>|</td><td>|</td><td>—</td><td>—</td><td>|</td><td>|</td><td>—</td><td>—</td><td>|</td><td>|</td><td>—</td><td>—</td><td>|</td><td>|</td><td>—</td><td>—</td><td>|</td><td>|</td><td>—</td><td>—</td><td>|</td><td>|</td><td>—</td><td>—</td><td>21</td></tr>
<tr><td>A</td><td>—</td><td>|</td><td>|</td><td>—</td><td>—</td><td>|</td><td>|</td><td>—</td><td>—</td><td>|</td><td>|</td><td>—</td><td>—</td><td>|</td><td>|</td><td>—</td><td>—</td><td>|</td><td>|</td><td>—</td><td>—</td><td>|</td><td>|</td><td>—</td><td>—</td><td>|</td><td>|</td><td>20</td></tr>
<tr><td>B</td><td>—</td><td>—</td><td>|</td><td>|</td><td>—</td><td>—</td><td>|</td><td>|</td><td>—</td><td>—</td><td>|</td><td>|</td><td>—</td><td>—</td><td>|</td><td>|</td><td>—</td><td>—</td><td>|</td><td>|</td><td>—</td><td>—</td><td>|</td><td>|</td><td>—</td><td>—</td><td>|</td><td>19</td></tr>
<tr><td>A</td><td>|</td><td>|</td><td>—</td><td>—</td><td>|</td><td>|</td><td>—</td><td>—</td><td>|</td><td>|</td><td>—</td><td>—</td><td>|</td><td>|</td><td>—</td><td>—</td><td>|</td><td>|</td><td>—</td><td>—</td><td>|</td><td>|</td><td>—</td><td>—</td><td>|</td><td>|</td><td>—</td><td>18</td></tr>
<tr><td>B</td><td>|</td><td>—</td><td>—</td><td>|</td><td>|</td><td>—</td><td>—</td><td>|</td><td>|</td><td>—</td><td>—</td><td>|</td><td>|</td><td>—</td><td>—</td><td>|</td><td>|</td><td>—</td><td>—</td><td>|</td><td>|</td><td>—</td><td>—</td><td>|</td><td>|</td><td>—</td><td>—</td><td>17</td></tr>
<tr><td>A</td><td>—</td><td>|</td><td>|</td><td>—</td><td>—</td><td>|</td><td>|</td><td>—</td><td>—</td><td>|</td><td>|</td><td>—</td><td>—</td><td>|</td><td>|</td><td>—</td><td>—</td><td>|</td><td>|</td><td>—</td><td>—</td><td>|</td><td>|</td><td>—</td><td>—</td><td>|</td><td>|</td><td>16</td></tr>
<tr><td>B</td><td>—</td><td>—</td><td>|</td><td>|</td><td>—</td><td>—</td><td>|</td><td>|</td><td>—</td><td>—</td><td>|</td><td>|</td><td>—</td><td>—</td><td>|</td><td>|</td><td>—</td><td>—</td><td>|</td><td>|</td><td>—</td><td>—</td><td>|</td><td>|</td><td>—</td><td>—</td><td>|</td><td>15</td></tr>
<tr><td>A</td><td>|</td><td>|</td><td>—</td><td>—</td><td>|</td><td>|</td><td>—</td><td>—</td><td>|</td><td>|</td><td>—</td><td>—</td><td>|</td><td>|</td><td>—</td><td>—</td><td>|</td><td>|</td><td>—</td><td>—</td><td>|</td><td>|</td><td>—</td><td>—</td><td>|</td><td>|</td><td>—</td><td>14</td></tr>
<tr><td>B</td><td>|</td><td>—</td><td>—</td><td>|</td><td>|</td><td>—</td><td>—</td><td>|</td><td>|</td><td>—</td><td>—</td><td>|</td><td>|</td><td>—</td><td>—</td><td>|</td><td>|</td><td>—</td><td>—</td><td>|</td><td>|</td><td>—</td><td>—</td><td>|</td><td>|</td><td>—</td><td>—</td><td>13</td></tr>
<tr><td>A</td><td>—</td><td>|</td><td>|</td><td>—</td><td>—</td><td>|</td><td>|</td><td>—</td><td>—</td><td>|</td><td>|</td><td>—</td><td>—</td><td>|</td><td>|</td><td>—</td><td>—</td><td>|</td><td>|</td><td>—</td><td>—</td><td>|</td><td>|</td><td>—</td><td>—</td><td>|</td><td>|</td><td>12</td></tr>
<tr><td>B</td><td>—</td><td>—</td><td>|</td><td>|</td><td>—</td><td>—</td><td>|</td><td>|</td><td>—</td><td>—</td><td>|</td><td>|</td><td>—</td><td>—</td><td>|</td><td>|</td><td>—</td><td>—</td><td>|</td><td>|</td><td>—</td><td>—</td><td>|</td><td>|</td><td>—</td><td>—</td><td>|</td><td>11</td></tr>
<tr><td>A</td><td>|</td><td>|</td><td>—</td><td>—</td><td>|</td><td>|</td><td>—</td><td>—</td><td>|</td><td>|</td><td>—</td><td>—</td><td>|</td><td>|</td><td>—</td><td>—</td><td>|</td><td>|</td><td>—</td><td>—</td><td>|</td><td>|</td><td>—</td><td>—</td><td>|</td><td>|</td><td>—</td><td>10</td></tr>
<tr><td>B</td><td>|</td><td>—</td><td>—</td><td>|</td><td>|</td><td>—</td><td>—</td><td>|</td><td>|</td><td>—</td><td>—</td><td>|</td><td>|</td><td>—</td><td>—</td><td>|</td><td>|</td><td>—</td><td>—</td><td>|</td><td>|</td><td>—</td><td>—</td><td>|</td><td>|</td><td>—</td><td>—</td><td>9</td></tr>
<tr><td>A</td><td>—</td><td>|</td><td>|</td><td>—</td><td>—</td><td>|</td><td>|</td><td>—</td><td>—</td><td>|</td><td>|</td><td>—</td><td>—</td><td>|</td><td>|</td><td>—</td><td>—</td><td>|</td><td>|</td><td>—</td><td>—</td><td>|</td><td>|</td><td>—</td><td>—</td><td>|</td><td>|</td><td>8</td></tr>
<tr><td>B</td><td>—</td><td>—</td><td>|</td><td>|</td><td>—</td><td>—</td><td>|</td><td>|</td><td>—</td><td>—</td><td>|</td><td>|</td><td>—</td><td>—</td><td>|</td><td>|</td><td>—</td><td>—</td><td>|</td><td>|</td><td>—</td><td>—</td><td>|</td><td>|</td><td>—</td><td>—</td><td>|</td><td>7</td></tr>
<tr><td>A</td><td>|</td><td>|</td><td>—</td><td>—</td><td>|</td><td>|</td><td>—</td><td>—</td><td>|</td><td>|</td><td>—</td><td>—</td><td>|</td><td>|</td><td>—</td><td>—</td><td>|</td><td>|</td><td>—</td><td>—</td><td>|</td><td>|</td><td>—</td><td>—</td><td>|</td><td>|</td><td>—</td><td>6</td></tr>
<tr><td>B</td><td>|</td><td>—</td><td>—</td><td>|</td><td>|</td><td>—</td><td>—</td><td>|</td><td>|</td><td>—</td><td>—</td><td>|</td><td>|</td><td>—</td><td>—</td><td>|</td><td>|</td><td>—</td><td>—</td><td>|</td><td>|</td><td>—</td><td>—</td><td>|</td><td>|</td><td>—</td><td>—</td><td>5</td></tr>
<tr><td>A</td><td>—</td><td>|</td><td>|</td><td>—</td><td>—</td><td>|</td><td>|</td><td>—</td><td>—</td><td>|</td><td>|</td><td>—</td><td>—</td><td>|</td><td>|</td><td>—</td><td>—</td><td>|</td><td>|</td><td>—</td><td>—</td><td>|</td><td>|</td><td>—</td><td>—</td><td>|</td><td>|</td><td>4</td></tr>
<tr><td>B</td><td>—</td><td>—</td><td>|</td><td>|</td><td>—</td><td>—</td><td>|</td><td>|</td><td>—</td><td>—</td><td>|</td><td>|</td><td>—</td><td>—</td><td>|</td><td>|</td><td>—</td><td>—</td><td>|</td><td>|</td><td>—</td><td>—</td><td>|</td><td>|</td><td>—</td><td>—</td><td>|</td><td>3</td></tr>
<tr><td>A</td><td>|</td><td>|</td><td>—</td><td>—</td><td>|</td><td>|</td><td>—</td><td>—</td><td>|</td><td>|</td><td>—</td><td>—</td><td>|</td><td>|</td><td>—</td><td>—</td><td>|</td><td>|</td><td>—</td><td>—</td><td>|</td><td>|</td><td>—</td><td>—</td><td>|</td><td>|</td><td>—</td><td>2</td></tr>
<tr><td>B</td><td>|</td><td>—</td><td>—</td><td>|</td><td>|</td><td>—</td><td>—</td><td>|</td><td>|</td><td>—</td><td>—</td><td>|</td><td>|</td><td>—</td><td>—</td><td>|</td><td>|</td><td>—</td><td>—</td><td>|</td><td>|</td><td>—</td><td>—</td><td>|</td><td>|</td><td>—</td><td>—</td><td>1</td></tr>
<tr><td></td><td>27</td><td>26</td><td>25</td><td>24</td><td>23</td><td>22</td><td>21</td><td>20</td><td>19</td><td>18</td><td>17</td><td>16</td><td>15</td><td>14</td><td>13</td><td>12</td><td>11</td><td>10</td><td>9</td><td>8</td><td>7</td><td>6</td><td>5</td><td>4</td><td>3</td><td>2</td><td>1</td><td></td></tr>
</table>

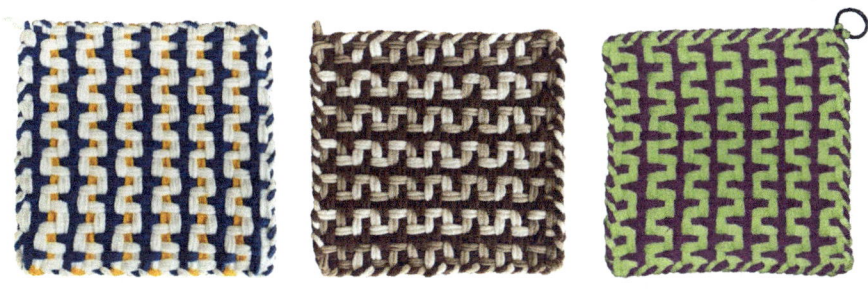

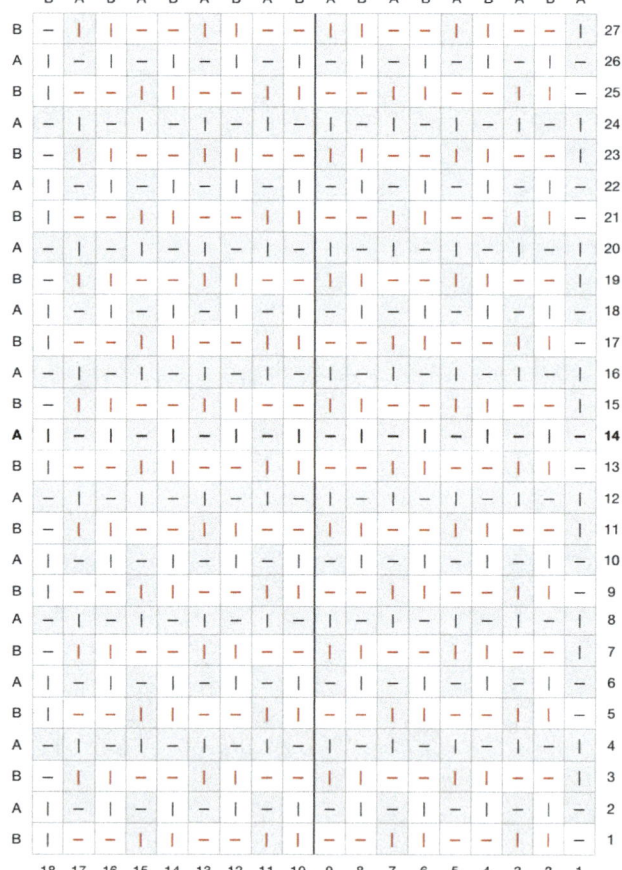

Greek Half Key

draft from handweaving.net, charted by Bill West

<table>
<tr><td></td><td>A</td><td>B</td><td>A</td><td>B</td><td>A</td><td>B</td><td>A</td><td>B</td><td>A</td><td>B</td><td>A</td><td>B</td><td>A</td><td>B</td><td>A</td><td>B</td><td>A</td><td>B</td><td>A</td><td>B</td><td>A</td><td>B</td><td>A</td><td>B</td><td>A</td><td>B</td><td>A</td><td></td></tr>
<tr><td>A</td><td>|</td><td>—</td><td>|</td><td>—</td><td>|</td><td>—</td><td>|</td><td>—</td><td>|</td><td>—</td><td>|</td><td>—</td><td>|</td><td>—</td><td>|</td><td>—</td><td>|</td><td>—</td><td>|</td><td>—</td><td>|</td><td>—</td><td>|</td><td>—</td><td>|</td><td>—</td><td>—</td><td>27</td></tr>
<tr><td>B</td><td>—</td><td>|</td><td>|</td><td>—</td><td>—</td><td>|</td><td>|</td><td>—</td><td>—</td><td>|</td><td>|</td><td>—</td><td>—</td><td>|</td><td>|</td><td>—</td><td>—</td><td>|</td><td>|</td><td>—</td><td>—</td><td>|</td><td>|</td><td>—</td><td>—</td><td>|</td><td>|</td><td>26</td></tr>
<tr><td>A</td><td>|</td><td>—</td><td>—</td><td>|</td><td>|</td><td>—</td><td>—</td><td>|</td><td>|</td><td>—</td><td>—</td><td>|</td><td>|</td><td>—</td><td>—</td><td>|</td><td>|</td><td>—</td><td>—</td><td>|</td><td>|</td><td>—</td><td>—</td><td>|</td><td>|</td><td>—</td><td>|</td><td>25</td></tr>
<tr><td>B</td><td>—</td><td>|</td><td>—</td><td>|</td><td>—</td><td>|</td><td>—</td><td>|</td><td>—</td><td>|</td><td>—</td><td>|</td><td>—</td><td>|</td><td>—</td><td>|</td><td>—</td><td>|</td><td>—</td><td>|</td><td>—</td><td>|</td><td>—</td><td>|</td><td>—</td><td>|</td><td>—</td><td>24</td></tr>
<tr><td>A</td><td>|</td><td>—</td><td>|</td><td>—</td><td>|</td><td>—</td><td>|</td><td>—</td><td>|</td><td>—</td><td>|</td><td>—</td><td>|</td><td>—</td><td>|</td><td>—</td><td>|</td><td>—</td><td>|</td><td>—</td><td>|</td><td>—</td><td>|</td><td>—</td><td>|</td><td>—</td><td>|</td><td>23</td></tr>
<tr><td>B</td><td>|</td><td>—</td><td>—</td><td>|</td><td>|</td><td>—</td><td>—</td><td>|</td><td>|</td><td>—</td><td>—</td><td>|</td><td>|</td><td>—</td><td>—</td><td>|</td><td>|</td><td>—</td><td>—</td><td>|</td><td>|</td><td>—</td><td>—</td><td>|</td><td>|</td><td>—</td><td>—</td><td>22</td></tr>
<tr><td>A</td><td>—</td><td>|</td><td>|</td><td>—</td><td>—</td><td>|</td><td>|</td><td>—</td><td>—</td><td>|</td><td>|</td><td>—</td><td>—</td><td>|</td><td>|</td><td>—</td><td>—</td><td>|</td><td>|</td><td>—</td><td>—</td><td>|</td><td>|</td><td>—</td><td>—</td><td>|</td><td>|</td><td>21</td></tr>
<tr><td>B</td><td>—</td><td>|</td><td>—</td><td>|</td><td>—</td><td>|</td><td>—</td><td>|</td><td>—</td><td>|</td><td>—</td><td>|</td><td>—</td><td>|</td><td>—</td><td>|</td><td>—</td><td>|</td><td>—</td><td>|</td><td>—</td><td>|</td><td>—</td><td>|</td><td>—</td><td>|</td><td>—</td><td>20</td></tr>
<tr><td>A</td><td>|</td><td>—</td><td>|</td><td>—</td><td>|</td><td>—</td><td>|</td><td>—</td><td>|</td><td>—</td><td>|</td><td>—</td><td>|</td><td>—</td><td>|</td><td>—</td><td>|</td><td>—</td><td>|</td><td>—</td><td>|</td><td>—</td><td>|</td><td>—</td><td>|</td><td>—</td><td>|</td><td>19</td></tr>
<tr><td>B</td><td>—</td><td>|</td><td>|</td><td>—</td><td>—</td><td>|</td><td>|</td><td>—</td><td>—</td><td>|</td><td>|</td><td>—</td><td>—</td><td>|</td><td>|</td><td>—</td><td>—</td><td>|</td><td>|</td><td>—</td><td>—</td><td>|</td><td>|</td><td>—</td><td>—</td><td>|</td><td>|</td><td>18</td></tr>
<tr><td>A</td><td>|</td><td>—</td><td>—</td><td>|</td><td>|</td><td>—</td><td>—</td><td>|</td><td>|</td><td>—</td><td>—</td><td>|</td><td>|</td><td>—</td><td>—</td><td>|</td><td>|</td><td>—</td><td>—</td><td>|</td><td>|</td><td>—</td><td>—</td><td>|</td><td>|</td><td>—</td><td>|</td><td>17</td></tr>
<tr><td>B</td><td>—</td><td>|</td><td>—</td><td>|</td><td>—</td><td>|</td><td>—</td><td>|</td><td>—</td><td>|</td><td>—</td><td>|</td><td>—</td><td>|</td><td>—</td><td>|</td><td>—</td><td>|</td><td>—</td><td>|</td><td>—</td><td>|</td><td>—</td><td>|</td><td>—</td><td>|</td><td>—</td><td>16</td></tr>
<tr><td>A</td><td>|</td><td>—</td><td>|</td><td>—</td><td>|</td><td>—</td><td>|</td><td>—</td><td>|</td><td>—</td><td>|</td><td>—</td><td>|</td><td>—</td><td>|</td><td>—</td><td>|</td><td>—</td><td>|</td><td>—</td><td>|</td><td>—</td><td>|</td><td>—</td><td>|</td><td>—</td><td>|</td><td>15</td></tr>
<tr><td>B</td><td>|</td><td>—</td><td>—</td><td>|</td><td>|</td><td>—</td><td>—</td><td>|</td><td>|</td><td>—</td><td>—</td><td>|</td><td>|</td><td>—</td><td>—</td><td>|</td><td>|</td><td>—</td><td>—</td><td>|</td><td>|</td><td>—</td><td>—</td><td>|</td><td>|</td><td>—</td><td>—</td><td>14</td></tr>
<tr><td>A</td><td>—</td><td>|</td><td>|</td><td>—</td><td>—</td><td>|</td><td>|</td><td>—</td><td>—</td><td>|</td><td>|</td><td>—</td><td>—</td><td>|</td><td>|</td><td>—</td><td>—</td><td>|</td><td>|</td><td>—</td><td>—</td><td>|</td><td>|</td><td>—</td><td>—</td><td>|</td><td>|</td><td>13</td></tr>
<tr><td>B</td><td>—</td><td>|</td><td>—</td><td>|</td><td>—</td><td>|</td><td>—</td><td>|</td><td>—</td><td>|</td><td>—</td><td>|</td><td>—</td><td>|</td><td>—</td><td>|</td><td>—</td><td>|</td><td>—</td><td>|</td><td>—</td><td>|</td><td>—</td><td>|</td><td>—</td><td>|</td><td>—</td><td>12</td></tr>
<tr><td>A</td><td>|</td><td>—</td><td>|</td><td>—</td><td>|</td><td>—</td><td>|</td><td>—</td><td>|</td><td>—</td><td>|</td><td>—</td><td>|</td><td>—</td><td>|</td><td>—</td><td>|</td><td>—</td><td>|</td><td>—</td><td>|</td><td>—</td><td>|</td><td>—</td><td>|</td><td>—</td><td>|</td><td>11</td></tr>
<tr><td>B</td><td>—</td><td>|</td><td>|</td><td>—</td><td>—</td><td>|</td><td>|</td><td>—</td><td>—</td><td>|</td><td>|</td><td>—</td><td>—</td><td>|</td><td>|</td><td>—</td><td>—</td><td>|</td><td>|</td><td>—</td><td>—</td><td>|</td><td>|</td><td>—</td><td>—</td><td>|</td><td>|</td><td>10</td></tr>
<tr><td>A</td><td>|</td><td>—</td><td>—</td><td>|</td><td>|</td><td>—</td><td>—</td><td>|</td><td>|</td><td>—</td><td>—</td><td>|</td><td>|</td><td>—</td><td>—</td><td>|</td><td>|</td><td>—</td><td>—</td><td>|</td><td>|</td><td>—</td><td>—</td><td>|</td><td>|</td><td>—</td><td>|</td><td>9</td></tr>
<tr><td>B</td><td>—</td><td>|</td><td>—</td><td>|</td><td>—</td><td>|</td><td>—</td><td>|</td><td>—</td><td>|</td><td>—</td><td>|</td><td>—</td><td>|</td><td>—</td><td>|</td><td>—</td><td>|</td><td>—</td><td>|</td><td>—</td><td>|</td><td>—</td><td>|</td><td>—</td><td>|</td><td>—</td><td>8</td></tr>
<tr><td>A</td><td>|</td><td>—</td><td>|</td><td>—</td><td>|</td><td>—</td><td>|</td><td>—</td><td>|</td><td>—</td><td>|</td><td>—</td><td>|</td><td>—</td><td>|</td><td>—</td><td>|</td><td>—</td><td>|</td><td>—</td><td>|</td><td>—</td><td>|</td><td>—</td><td>|</td><td>—</td><td>|</td><td>7</td></tr>
<tr><td>B</td><td>|</td><td>—</td><td>—</td><td>|</td><td>|</td><td>—</td><td>—</td><td>|</td><td>|</td><td>—</td><td>—</td><td>|</td><td>|</td><td>—</td><td>—</td><td>|</td><td>|</td><td>—</td><td>—</td><td>|</td><td>|</td><td>—</td><td>—</td><td>|</td><td>|</td><td>—</td><td>—</td><td>6</td></tr>
<tr><td>A</td><td>—</td><td>|</td><td>|</td><td>—</td><td>—</td><td>|</td><td>|</td><td>—</td><td>—</td><td>|</td><td>|</td><td>—</td><td>—</td><td>|</td><td>|</td><td>—</td><td>—</td><td>|</td><td>|</td><td>—</td><td>—</td><td>|</td><td>|</td><td>—</td><td>—</td><td>|</td><td>|</td><td>5</td></tr>
<tr><td>B</td><td>—</td><td>|</td><td>—</td><td>|</td><td>—</td><td>|</td><td>—</td><td>|</td><td>—</td><td>|</td><td>—</td><td>|</td><td>—</td><td>|</td><td>—</td><td>|</td><td>—</td><td>|</td><td>—</td><td>|</td><td>—</td><td>|</td><td>—</td><td>|</td><td>—</td><td>|</td><td>—</td><td>4</td></tr>
<tr><td>A</td><td>|</td><td>—</td><td>|</td><td>—</td><td>|</td><td>—</td><td>|</td><td>—</td><td>|</td><td>—</td><td>|</td><td>—</td><td>|</td><td>—</td><td>|</td><td>—</td><td>|</td><td>—</td><td>|</td><td>—</td><td>|</td><td>—</td><td>|</td><td>—</td><td>|</td><td>—</td><td>|</td><td>3</td></tr>
<tr><td>B</td><td>—</td><td>|</td><td>|</td><td>—</td><td>—</td><td>|</td><td>|</td><td>—</td><td>—</td><td>|</td><td>|</td><td>—</td><td>—</td><td>|</td><td>|</td><td>—</td><td>—</td><td>|</td><td>|</td><td>—</td><td>—</td><td>|</td><td>|</td><td>—</td><td>—</td><td>|</td><td>|</td><td>2</td></tr>
<tr><td>A</td><td>|</td><td>—</td><td>—</td><td>|</td><td>|</td><td>—</td><td>—</td><td>|</td><td>|</td><td>—</td><td>—</td><td>|</td><td>|</td><td>—</td><td>—</td><td>|</td><td>|</td><td>—</td><td>—</td><td>|</td><td>|</td><td>—</td><td>—</td><td>|</td><td>|</td><td>—</td><td>|</td><td>1</td></tr>
<tr><td></td><td>27</td><td>26</td><td>25</td><td>24</td><td>23</td><td>22</td><td>21</td><td>20</td><td>19</td><td>18</td><td>17</td><td>16</td><td>15</td><td>14</td><td>13</td><td>12</td><td>11</td><td>10</td><td>9</td><td>8</td><td>7</td><td>6</td><td>5</td><td>4</td><td>3</td><td>2</td><td>1</td><td></td></tr>
</table>

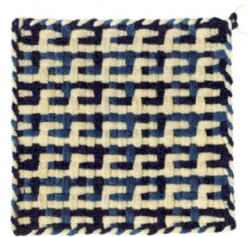

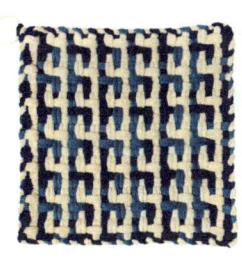

CHAPTER 6

a somewhat nerdy log cabin study

The history of Log Cabin goes back at least as far as Neolithic central and western Europe (4,500 to 500 BCE), where an example of the pattern was found in a pile-dwellers' archeological site. (Reference: E. J. W. Barber, "Prehistoric Textiles") I couldn't find a photo of the textile fragment, and would love to see it! We weave the traditional Log Cabin by warping a sequence of two alternating colors, repeating the sequence reversed, and repeating the whole for the width of your loom. Weft then follows the warp sequence. From this rule have come some of our strongest classic patterns: all the variations of pinwheel (also known as puppytooth), the log cabin itself, and more.

In mathematics, one way to find out how many ways to arrange objects in a given number (n) of places is a simple permutation. The log cabin rule uses two colors: light and dark. So we'd use the formula 2 (for the colors A and B) to the power of n: 2^n.

What happens if you systematically permute the light and dark colors of the log cabin pattern from 2 places through 5 places, and then apply the rule? A sequence of repeating motifs come and go; are rotated, or displaced up, down, to the right or to the left. Take a look: you might find a new favorite.

2^2

2^2 = 4: There are 4 permutations of A and B in two places: AA, BB, AB, and BA. For each, we first write the sequence, and then reverse it.

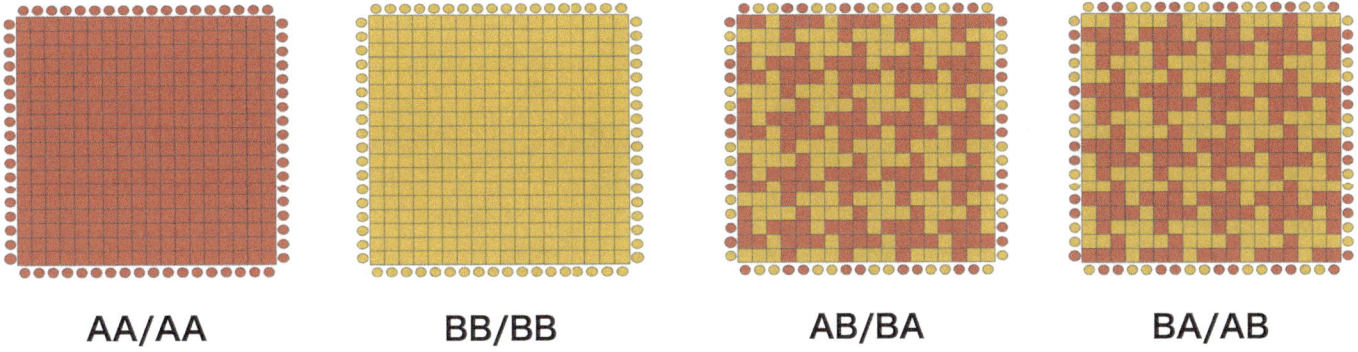

Since AA/AA and BB/BB don't meet the two-color requirement, they're eliminated as log cabin. We're left with AB/BA and BA/AB — but these are the same:

AB/BA —> ABBAABBAABBAABBAAB

BA/AB —>   BAABBAABBAABBAAB

If you look closely, you'll see that if BA/AB is turned upside down (rotated 180 degrees) you get AB/BA.

We get 3 distinct potholders from 4 permutations, and we get 1 potholder that meets the log cabin rule. This is Pinwheel, also known as Puppytooth, because it is the most basic form of the houndstooth pattern.

2^3

2^3 = 8: There are 8 permutations of A and B in three places: AAA, BBB, AAB, BAA, ABB, BBA, ABA, and BAB.

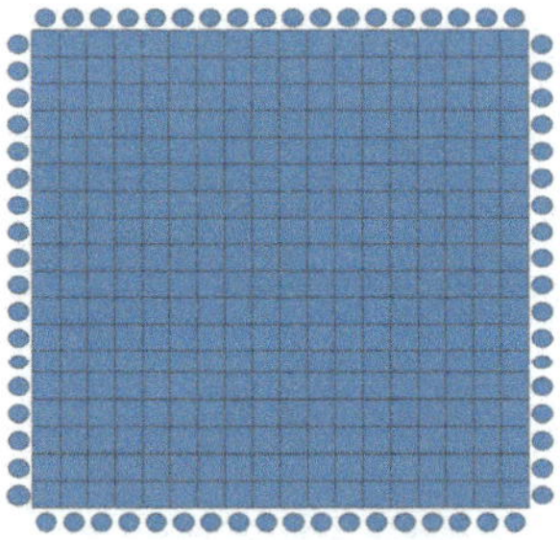

AAA/AAA
doesn't meet rule

AAB/BAA
BAA/AAB

AAB/BAA —> AABBAAAABBAAAABBAA
BAA/AAB —>   BAAAABBAAAABBAA

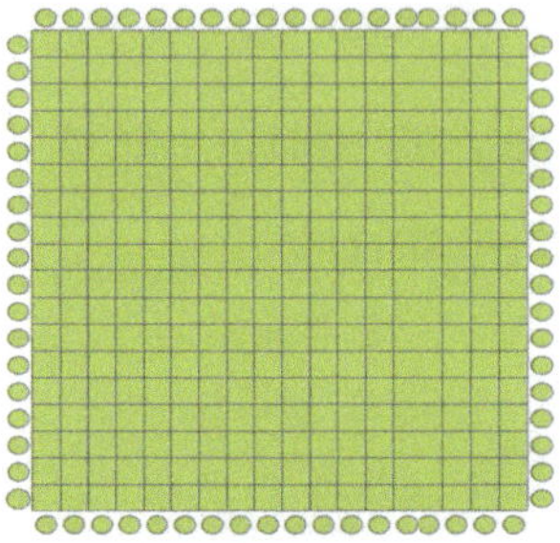

BBB/BBB
doesn't meet rule

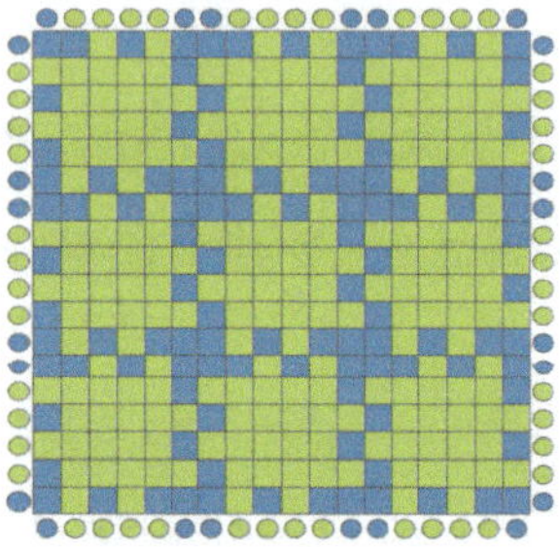

BBA/ABA
BBA/ABB

ABB/BBA —> ABBBBAABBBBAABBBBA
BBA/ABB —>   BBAABBBBAABBBBA

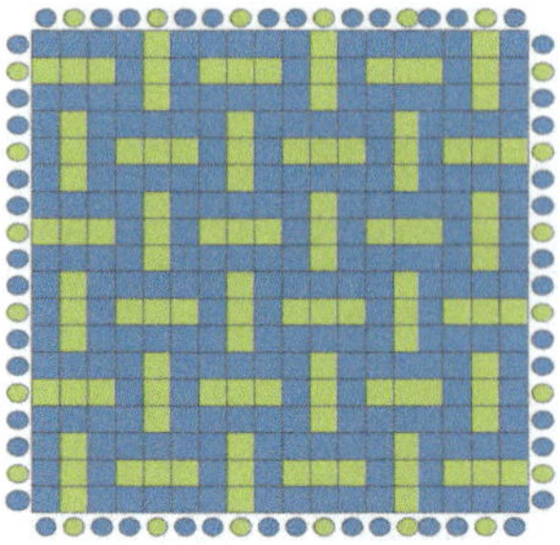

ABA/ABA

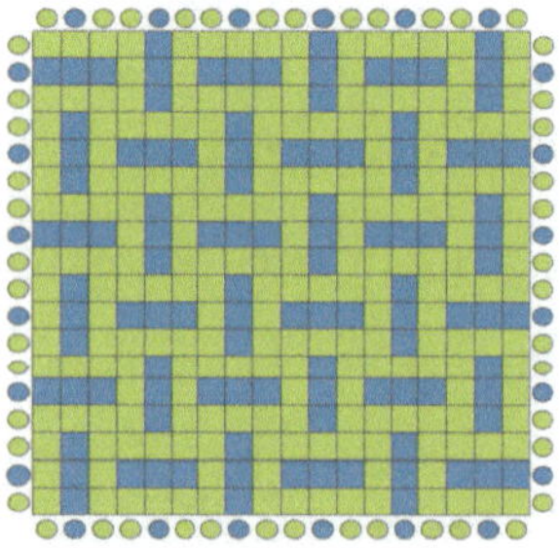

BAB/BAB

These two are simply color reversals.

Again we eliminate AAA and BBB. Two sets of permutations are the same, and another two are color reversals. We get 6 distinct potholders from 8 permutations, and we get 3 log cabin patterns.

2^4

2^4 = 16: There are 16 permutations of A and B in four places: AAAA, BBBB, ABAA, AABA, BABB, BBAB, AAAB, BAAA, ABBB, BBBA, AABB, BBAA, ABBA, BAAB, ABAB, and BABA.

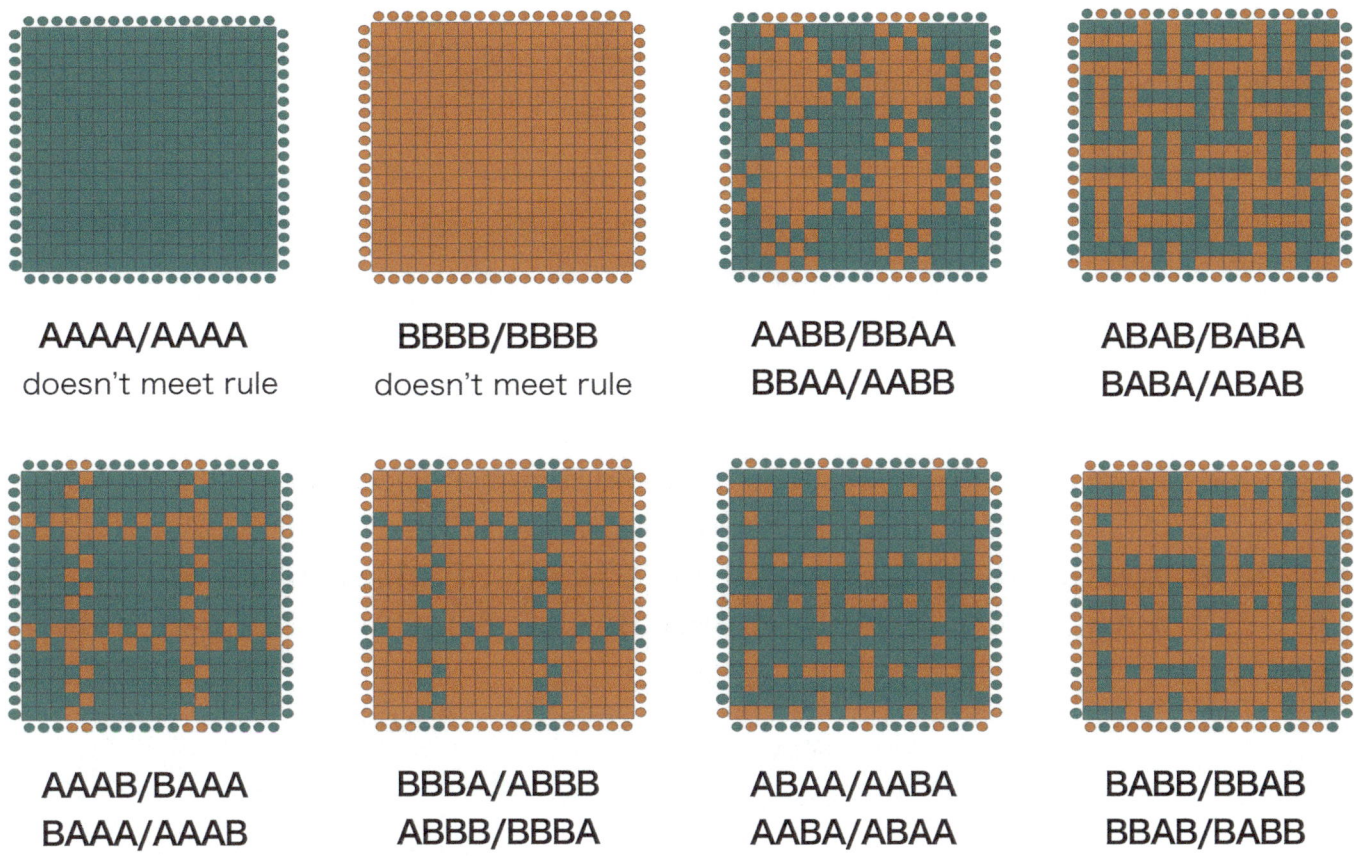

AAAA/AAAA
doesn't meet rule

BBBB/BBBB
doesn't meet rule

AABB/BBAA
BBAA/AABB

ABAB/BABA
BABA/ABAB

AAAB/BAAA
BAAA/AAAB

BBBA/ABBB
ABBB/BBBA

ABAA/AABA
AABA/ABAA

BABB/BBAB
BBAB/BABB

These are color reversals.

These are color reversals.

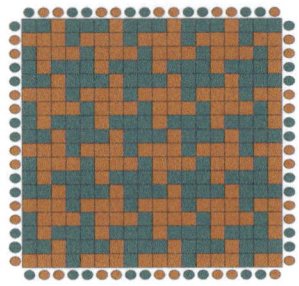

ABBA/ABBA —> ABBAABBAABBAABBAAB
BAAB/BAAB —> BAABBAABBAABBAAB
AB/BA —> ABBAABBAABBAAB
This is the same as AB/BA, Pinwheel, so we won't count it twice.

ABBA/ABBA
BAAB/BAAB

We get 9 distinct potholders from 16 permutations, and we get 5 log cabin patterns.

2^5

2^5 = 32: There are 32 permutations of A and B in five places: AAAAA, BBBBB, AAAAB, BAAAA, BBBBA, ABBBB, AAABA, ABAAA, BBBAB, BABBB, AABAA, BBABB, AAABB, BBAAA, AABBB, BBBAA, AABAB, BABAA, BBABA, ABABB, BABBA, ABBAB, AABBA, ABBAA, BBABB, BAABB, ABBBA, BAAAB, ABABA, BABAB, ABABB, and BAABA.

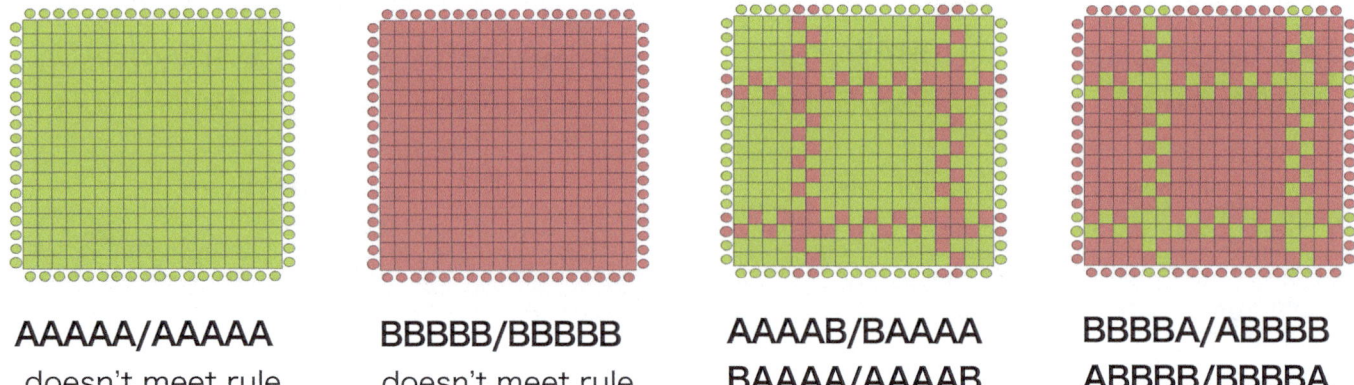

AAAAA/AAAAA
doesn't meet rule

BBBBB/BBBBB
doesn't meet rule

AAAAB/BAAAA
BAAAA/AAAAB

BBBBA/ABBBB
ABBBB/BBBBA

These are color reversals.

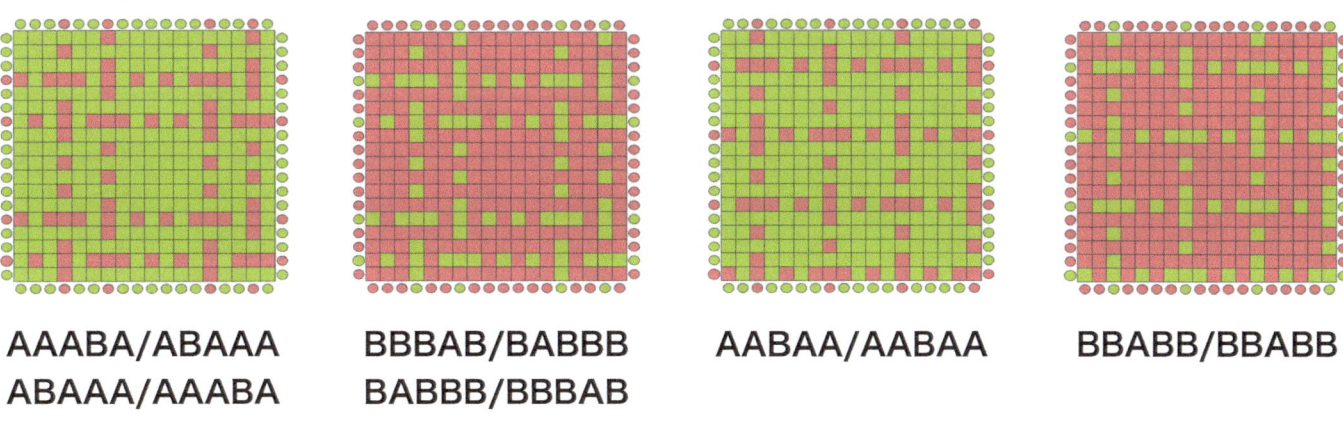

AAABA/ABAAA
ABAAA/AAABA

BBBAB/BABBB
BABBB/BBBAB

AABAA/AABAA

BBABB/BBABB

These are color reversals.

These are color reversals.

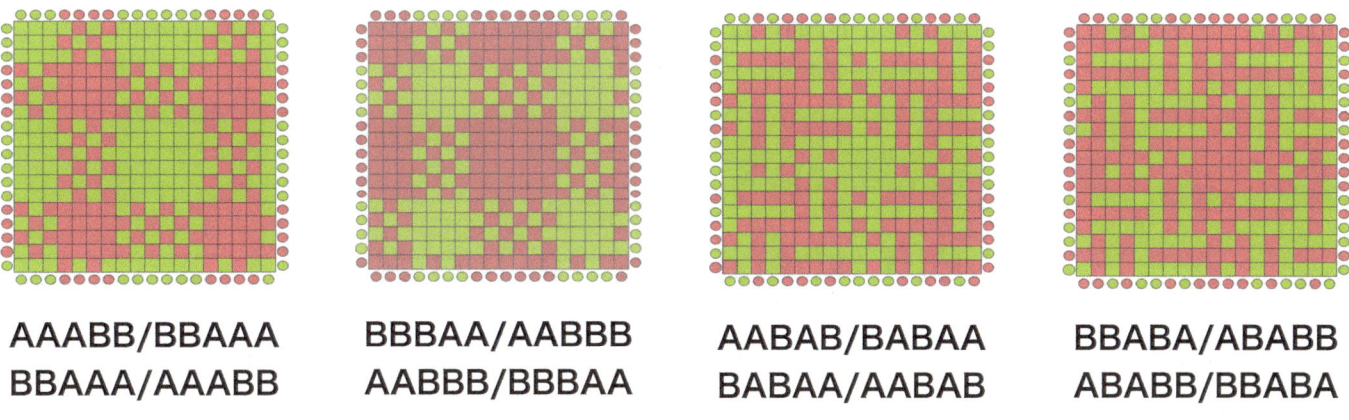

AAABB/BBAAA
BBAAA/AAABB

BBBAA/AABBB
AABBB/BBBAA

AABAB/BABAA
BABAA/AABAB

BBABA/ABABB
ABABB/BBABA

These are color reversals.

These are color reversals.

BABBA/ABBAB
ABBAB/BABBA

AABBA/ABBAA
ABBAA/AABBA

BBAAB/BAABB
BAABB/BBAAB

These are color reversals.

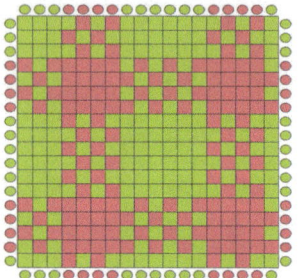 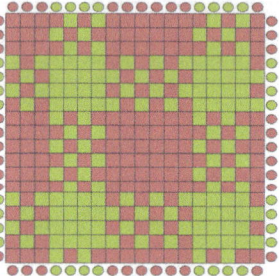 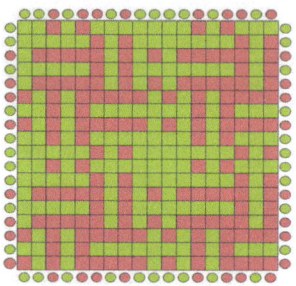 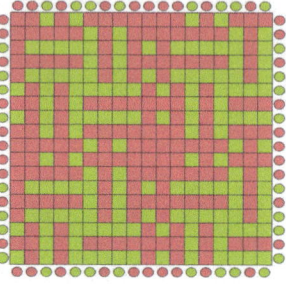

AAABB/BBAAA BBAAA/AAABB	BBBAA/AABBB AABBB/BBBAA	AABAB/BABAA BABAA/AABAB	BBABA/ABABB ABABB/BBABA

These are color reversals.　　　　　　　　These are color reversals.

We get 19 distinct potholders from 32 permutations, and we get 9 log cabin patterns.

But where are the logs?

....you might ask. The most common log cabin looks like stacked logs, and is warped (and woven) with alternating light/dark colors. So the notation would be written ABAB for as far as you like, and then reversed, per the log cabin rule. As the length of the sequence increases past 5, the logs become more recognizable.

Here are those from the above permutation sets:

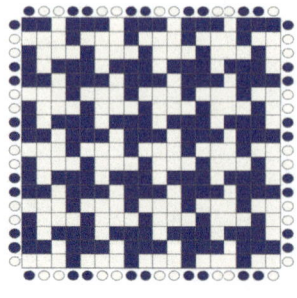  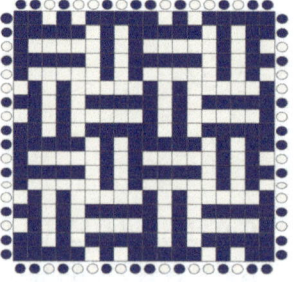 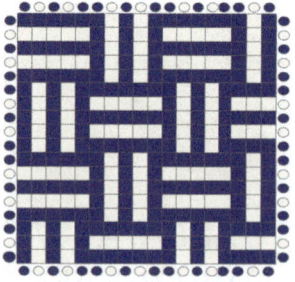

AB/BA　　　　　ABA/ABA　　　　　ABAB/BABA　　　　ABABA/ABABA
　　　　　　　　　　　　　　　　　(centered)

Here are the others, up to the limit of an 18-peg loom:

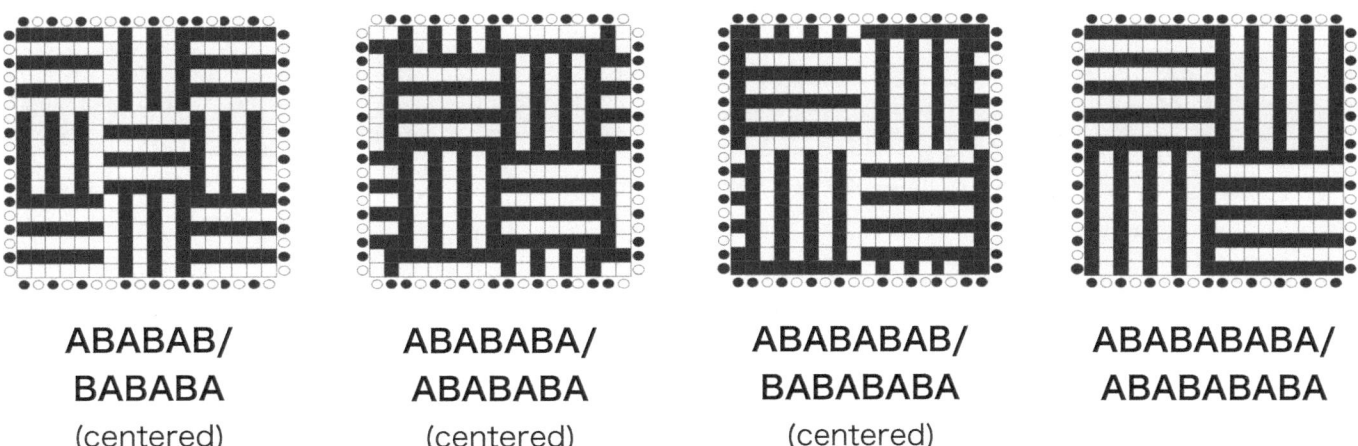

ABABAB/
BABABA
(centered)

ABABABA/
ABABABA
(centered)

ABABABAB/
BABABABA
(centered)

ABABABABA/
ABABABABA

The Log Cabin Rule: Log Cabin is woven by warping a sequence of two alternating colors, repeating the sequence reversed, and repeating the whole for the width of your loom. Weft follows the warp sequence.

CHAPTER 7

potholder weavers

There are no potholders without potholder weavers. And there are no potholders that catch your eye, startle you, make you want to hang them up on the wall, and change your mind about what a potholder is and can be, without potholder weavers with vision. These potholder weavers look at a simple loom and see possibility; they take the loom in hand and weave a transformation. From our most cherished traditional patterns to the completely original, potholder weavers move this most simple, practical craft forward, exploring color and structure.

It's both a small adventure and a large one. People like potholders, it seems. A strong pattern is continually pleasant to look at, and, since a potholder has a necessary, practical use in the kitchen as hand protection or trivet, it's always there to brighten a moment. Weaving these small textiles is relaxing, simple, interesting, fairly quick, and fun. Working with color and weave structure is fascinating, and expressive: something inside is released into a freedom when you make one — that's the creativity that every person has, that makes potholders so satisfying. Then, you can give them away and make other people happy.

The weavers in this chapter are those that have helped with this book, or who have supported this crazy effort: they converted patterns from 4-harness loom drafts, invented original patterns, test wove them, had encouraging words to say, and together inspired creative breakthrough. I hope they inspire you, and that their work sparks your own innate creativity.

Bill West

I'm a native Tennessean living on the outskirts of Nashville. I've resided in this area most of my life other than when I lived in NYC during the late 80s and early 90s.

My career started with a major clothing manufacturer working as a pattern maker. I took the designer's sample garment along with a clothing specification sheet and graded (made) a complete size range of patterns from her designs to be used at our sewing factories. After eight years of making patterns I changed positions and was the trim buyer, purchasing all trim items (thread, buttons, fasteners, zippers, etc.) for the twenty sewing factories.

In the late 80s I moved to New York City and worked in the garment district as a production coordinator for a children's clothing manufacturer doing cost analysis and scheduling production for the factories.

I returned to Nashville in 1993 and decided it was time for a complete career change. I went to work at a major telecommunication corporation and retired as a Compliance Manager after 24 years.

Like many others I made potholders as a kid. Last year when the pandemic began, bored out of my mind, knowing I needed something to keep my sanity, I rediscovered the art of making potholders. I looked online and ordered the traditional loom. Before the loom arrived, I saw there was now a loom that took 10 inch loops so I immediately ordered that one along with a bulk 5# bag of loops.

I knew the traditional size loom and style potholders would never keep my interest so I started looking on Pinterest for updated looks. I did find several styles different from what I had known as a child, but no patterns. I would figure out what I needed to do to recreate that style and also convert to make them on a 27 peg loom using 10 inch loops. At the same time while recreating the new found styles, I decided to make templates in Excel so I could use the pattern for when I made the style again. On Pinterest I started seeing weaving drafts for fabrics with designs which made me think, "Can I chart a potholder using these drafts?" The answer to that was "Yes, some you can and some you can't." So not only was I challenging myself with making potholders with a new look, I was also challenging myself by making patterns for these. At that time I decided I would label my potholders 'Ain't your Granny's Potholder.'

I am happy to contribute several of my patterns to this amazing book and hope that everyone enjoys making potholders from all of the patterns in the book. I'm sure when things return to some sense of normalcy, my potholder and pattern making will slow down, but I will probably always dabble in the art.

One thing I hope everyone learns from this is: step outside of your box and away from your comfort zone as there are possibilities waiting for you to discover.

Instagram: @aintyourgrannyspotholder

Mary Clarke

When it comes to making potholders, I try to stay true to their humble nature. For me, that means:

• A traditional 18 or 19-peg loom. The dimensions of the classic 6-inch square potholder are perfect, no matter the size of your hands.

• Plain weaves and simple motifs. Of late, I alternate between brain-teasing linear patterns like Right-Angle Hitch and more meditative, abstract, off-center designs.

• A considered approach to color. I tend to reach for reds and various shades of blue — like potholders of yore — but also pinks, ochre, leaf green and burgundy. And I'm still searching for the perfect light blue. (A few colors rarely used: purple, emerald or lime green, or gray.)

• Neutrals add modernity and are perfect for offsetting vibrant hues, but moderation is key. Only one or two neutrals allowed — any more than that, and you lose the spirit of the potholder. At their best, they are stealthy little color bombs.

- Two colors are good, three are often better. It is rare that I use more than four.

About me: I'm a longtime magazine editor, born and raised and living in New York City. Though I trace my earliest potholder-making efforts to nursery school, it's only in the last 10 or so years that I've become a more devoted looper, sharing much of my work with family and friends.

My potholders have been exhibited in "Cloth Made More Interesting by People" at Feature Inc. gallery in New York City and at artist Rob Pruitt's Holiday Flea Market at Karma Bookstore. Some of my potholders can be seen on Instagram at **@maryksee**.

Christine Olsen Reis

Born into an Alaskan halibut and black cod fishing family, I was steeped in the natural world from my youth and found artistic inspiration in the sea, sky and forest.

I began weaving in my late teens. Captivated and inspired by excellent teachers and a love of finding patterns, my early work was with Northwest Coastal textiles, basketry and Swedish loom weaving. I studied at California College of the Arts graduating with an Art and Art History degree from Western Washington University and an MFA from the University of Washington in Fiber Arts. That lead to practicing and teaching art and design. Indigenous textiles, powerful pattern design and finding beauty and meaning in art and nature are my current passion.

Instagram: @creiscreate

Foghorns

I am **Yavia Mirez** and I live in the unique village of Hell, Michigan. Yes, that is its real name! Before you ask, yes, it does freeze over. I have the best job ever. I am the Official Minister Of Hell's Chapel of Love and officiate wedding ceremonies all year round. Your marriage license will actually say Married in Hell.

We have a lot of fun with the village's name and promote a fun family friendly community filled with lakes, hiking trails and year round events.

I am a crocheter, circular knitter, and rock painter. I've recently added loom potholder maker to my list after a 52 year hiatus! I have rekindled the happiness that making these items brings! The designs and colors are much more fascinating and kicked up then when I was 8 when I learned to make them.

The amazing thing about today's potholders, mug rugs and trivet pads is that they are 100% cotton or wool and best of all, usable! No need to hide these away!

I tell my family I've gone "Loopy" lately — but not to worry it's a good loopy!

Angela West

I worked in the telecommunications industry for over 30 years. I have always been an outdoor type person. My hobbies include golfing, cycling, hiking when the weather permits in Nashville, Tennessee.

I consider myself a novice weaver compared to the other weavers in this book. I began weaving during the pandemic to have a project to work on as things closed. Potholder weaving has become my creative therapy, almost like meditation.

My brother Bill West and I both started this together — he has become a master at charting and creating patterns. We have both learned and improved tremendously since we started. We both continue to make mistakes on weaves, but we have laughed so hard it has brought us to tears...that's been the best part! Have fun and keep on weaving!

'Wavy Zigzag'

H. Michelle Spaulding

I am a certified dream coach, teacher, an expressive arts facilitator, visionary artist, author and storyteller. I express myself through the textile and fiber arts. I teach

workshops to women who want to express their creativity through crafting and art making. I left the corporate world after twenty years as Founder and CEO of a high tech firm in the government contracting arena to pursue a second career in Expressive Arts Education.

My latest crafting obsession is weaving potholders and making baskets and journals out of them. My weaving style is 'freestyle' or intuitive. I don't follow patterns. I look at patterns for inspiration but when I sit down to weave I go with the flow. Weaving is a Spiritual practice for me. I weave as a form of active meditation. Making and creating allows me to tap into the Divine creativity of our Universal force. I find that making baskets, totes, purses, journals etc. from handwoven potholders spiritually rewarding.

www.Craftydivacottage.com

dream create manifest

Crafty Diva
dream coaching

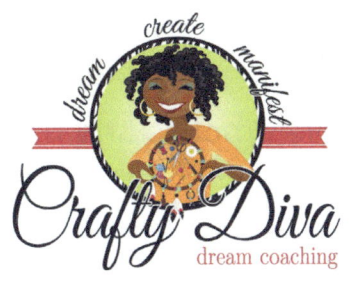

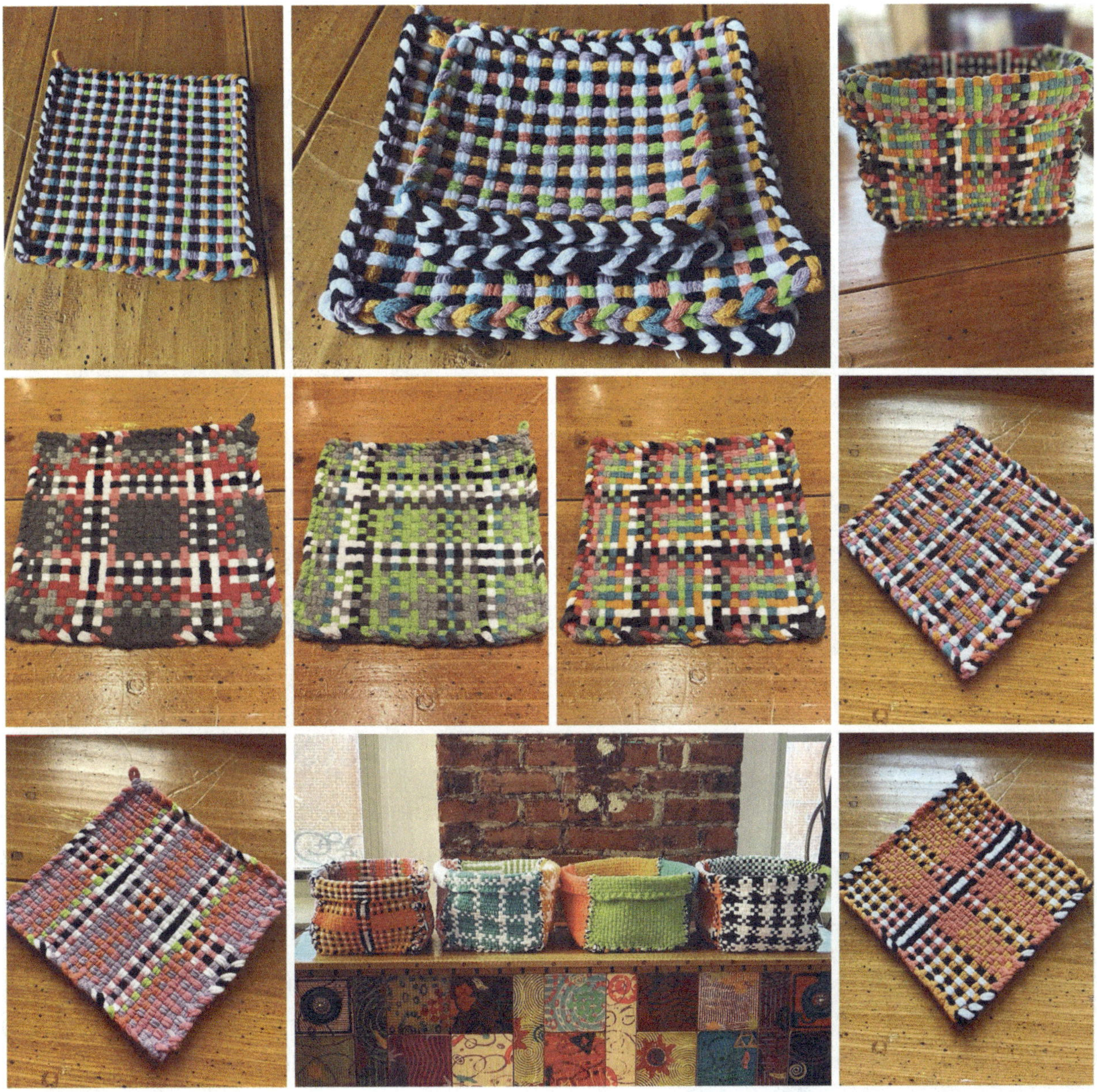

Kate Kilmurray

I had been practicing and teaching yoga and meditation for more than thirty years before unearthing a forgotten item from my childhood that sparked an immediate connection between my meditative practice and using our hands in craft. Holding a simple 7 x 7 inch metal handloom, I remembered my grandmother's hands teaching me to weave and I realized my introduction to meditation had happened as a child, weaving on a handloom.

When I rediscovered weaving through these evocative memories, I remembered something that we, as a culture, have forgotten: that we can always access inner stillness and peace through

simple, embodied practices. Handweaving as meditation has been a way of life for me ever since.

Understanding this connection has allowed me to be part of a community of women who are pioneering a new terrain of weaving; transforming something that has previously been thought of as an activity for children into a medium that has depth and presence for the 21st Century.

By using our hands in craft and contemplation, we can quiet the mind and reconnect with ourselves, something which is sorely needed in our technology-saturated world.

In 2020, I created The Weaving Way Community, an online group of now over 80 members across the US who all share a passion and interest for this style of weaving. This connection with my fellow members helps to drive my innovation in handweaving and my designs emerge from spacious and quiet communion with the colors, textures, and patterns of the natural world. Weaving in this way has led me to running a successful business selling my weaving designs across the world, as well as teaching others to weave as a meditative experience.
I believe that by incorporating handweavings in our homes, we bring more depth, beauty, and meaning to our daily lives. Weaving as meditation is a process of remembering who we are.

Instagram: @katekilmurray
www.katekilmurray.com

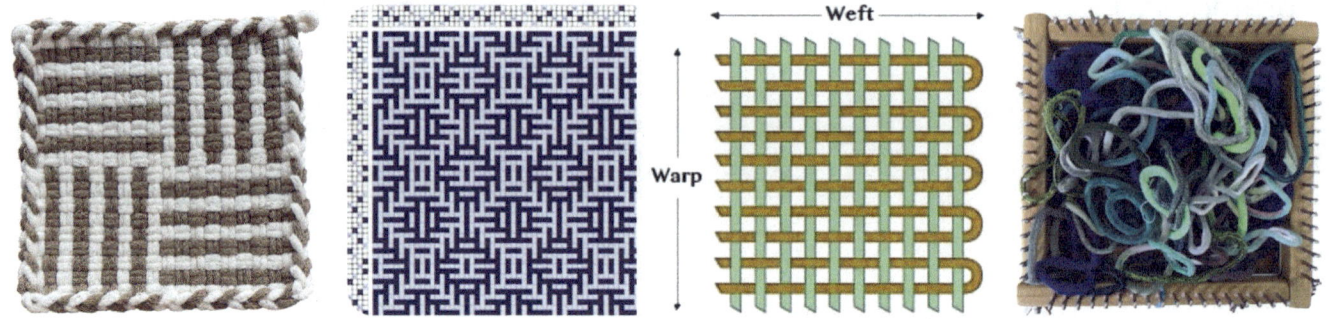

GLOSSARY

Color-and-weave: a broad classification in which the pattern effect is a result of both a weave structure and the sequence of contrasting warp and weft loops.

Log Cabin: the most basic shadow weave effect, where the alternating sequence of dark and light loops look like logs. Log Cabin is woven by warping a sequence of two alternating colors, repeating the sequence reversed, and repeating the whole for the width of your loom. Weft follows the warp sequence.

Pick: a. moving the weft loop over or under a warp loop; b. properly, one pass of the weft through the shed.

Plain weave: a basic weave structure where the weft alternates over and under the warp. It's also called tabby.

Shadow weave: a color-and-weave effect with a combination structure of plain weave and a twill-step at pattern changes. Two adjacent colors shadow each other.

Shed: the gap that occurs when you separate your warp loops into upper and lower.

Shrinkage: how much the fabric shrinks after washing. As a rule of thumb, cotton shrinks 10%, wool 15%, and synthetics (in general) 10%.

Take-up: how much the yarn rebounds after being removed from the loom. If your weft loops lay fairly loose across the loom, tension will be less, and takeup will be less: your potholder will lay flatter. Tug your loops.

Twill: a weave structure where the weft passes over or under one or more warp loops, then over or under two or more warp loops and so on, with a "step" or offset, between rows. The offset creates the diagonal look of a twill.

Warp: the vertical loops on a loom.

Weave structure: the manner in which the warp and weft interlace, as in plain weave, twill, basket weave, satin weave.

Weaving draft: a graphic representation of how to set your loom up to weave the pattern shown on the draft. The parts of the draft — threading, treadling, tie-up, and drawdown — tell the weaver how to warp their loom, and what the pattern will look like.

Weft: the horizontal loops which are woven over and under the warp loops.

PATTERN LIST

A
Apollo's Lyre p. 64

B
Bernie's Mitts p. 57
Birds Flying High p. 126
Box Chains p. 60
Boxed Angles p. 66
Broken Comb p. 32
Broken Ladders p. 34

C
Catherine Wheels p. 44
Christine's Garden Sampler p. 58
Circuitboard p. 65
Comb p. 36
Comb Variation p.38
Confetti p. 46
Corners p. 62

D
Diamond Burst p. 128
Diamond Mix p. 130
Diamond Repeat p. 132
Diamond Rose p. 134
Diamond Twill p. 136
Diamonds Are Forever p. 138

E
Equals p. 56
Escape p. 68
Exposed Filmstrips p. 140

F
Facets p. 70
Fillet p. 72
Film Strips p. 48
Four Corners p. 74

G
Garden Path p. 142
Greek Courtyard p. 76
Greek Half Key p. 159

I
Infinite p. 78

K
Kantha p. 30

L
Ladders p. 40
Little Squares/Thor's Hammer p. 144
Log Cabin ABA/BAB p. 42
Looking Through Barred Windows p. 80
Loop de Loop p. 82

M
Maze in a Diamond p. 84
Maze of Enigma p. 85
Multicursal Maze p. 86

O
Opening p. 88

P
Pi p. 27
Pinwheel aka Puppy Tooth p. 50
Prism Twill p. 129

R
Ramble p. 90
Right Angles p. 92
Right-angle Hitch p. 94

S
Scattered Twill (Broken Twill) p. 146
Shadow Aztec p. 96
Shadow Baseball Diamond p. 98
Shadow Cross p. 81
Shadow Diamond p. 75
Shadow Fern p. 100
Shadow Kelp p. 102
Shadow Seaweed p.106
Shadow Seaweed 2 p. 104
Shadow Seaweed 3 p. 105
Shadow X p. 108
Shadow Zigzag p. 110
Shine Bright Like a Diamond p. 148
Shuriken p. 150
Spider Woman's Cross p. 112
Spiral Maze p. 124
Square Maze p. 122
Square-in-a-Square p. 114
Straight-edged Spiral p. 116
Stripes p. 28

T
T p. 52
Twill X p. 152

U
Up the Down Staircase p. 147

V
Vessel III p. 111

W
Wavy Chevron Twill p. 154
Wavy Zigzag, Top Left p. 118
Wavy Zigzag, Top Right p. 119
Wavy Zigzag, Bottom Left p. 120
Wavy Zigzag, Bottom Right p. 121
Wiggle Worms p. 156

Z
Zipper p. 54